HUMAN RIGHTS AND ELECTIONS

A Handbook on International Human Rights Standards on Elections

UNITED NATIONS
HUMAN RIGHTS
OFFICE OF THE HIGH COMMISSIONER

Professional Training Series No. 2/Rev.1

New York and Geneva, 2021

United Nations publication, issued by the Office of the United Nations High Commissioner for Human Rights (OHCHR).

HR/P/PT/2/Rev. 1
ISBN: 978-92-1-154236-3
eISBN: 978-92-1-403052-2
Sales No.: E.21.XIV.3
ISSN (print): 1020-1688
ISSN (electronic): 2412-1398

Cover photo credit: UN Photo/Logan Abassi

CONTENTS

FOREWORD

People's right to participate in the conduct of public affairs is a fundamental imperative. Genuine and credible elections remain the most compelling and effective way for people to participate in governance and have their voices heard. Elections empower citizens to express their will and help to build or consolidate sustainable democracies.

The first edition of *Human Rights and Elections: A Handbook on the Legal, Technical and Human Rights Aspects of Elections* was published nearly three decades ago. Since then, the human rights landscape has shifted. New international treaties, such as the Convention on the Rights of Persons with Disabilities, have acknowledged the rights of people long marginalized. United Nations human rights mechanisms have issued jurisprudence clarifying States' obligations and advancing the right to vote and related rights.

At the same time, new challenges to participatory rights and the integrity of elections have emerged, such as hate speech, Internet blocking or disinformation campaigns, which are often facilitated or propagated by new technologies.

So, we emphatically celebrate the advancement of women in politics and the increasing focus on participation by people with disabilities, people of African descent, indigenous peoples, members of minority communities and other marginalized groups.

However, progress to date is far from sufficient. We will therefore continue to call for the eradication of severe and structural discrimination, which harms millions of people, creating obstacles to their equal participation and pushing them further behind.

Genuine and credible elections are nourished by a complex ecosystem made up of interlocking human rights protections: the impartial rule of law; and respect for fundamental freedoms and essential rights, such as education, which empower people to make free and informed choices. In other words, respect for civil, political, economic, social and cultural rights is an essential part of any electoral process – and the present handbook shows how human rights norms and standards are applicable to various aspects of elections.

Today, after a period of increased democratization around the world, many democracies appear to be backsliding. Some Governments seem to be deliberately weakening independent checks on their powers, suffocating criticism, dismantling democratic oversight and ensuring their long-term rule.

The power of technology is frequently harnessed to serve this effort, with intense surveillance of people's actions and speech, and disinformation campaigns that undermine the integrity of elections. These challenges create a heightened sense of urgency for those who work to advance the right to participate in public affairs. We must come together to find ways to engage as directly and forcefully as possible, strengthen the approaches that work, and reach out towards new avenues and partnerships.

In that context, I want to emphasize the enormous body of work that has already been done to ensure that human rights law can deliver a tested framework to assess online conduct and guide States' responses. The handbook includes a summary of that work to date.

Elections underpin the legitimacy of Governments and political leaders. Against a backdrop of respect for human rights norms, elections help to build States and Governments that are strong and legitimate because they demonstrate respect for their people and empower them to express their will.

Speaking as both the United Nations High Commissioner for Human Rights, and as a former elected Head of State and Government, I hope the handbook will serve as a useful tool for your efforts to promote genuine and credible elections around the world.

Michelle Bachelet
United Nations High Commissioner
for Human Rights

INTRODUCTION

1. Elections lie at the heart of democracy and remain the primary means through which individuals exercise their right to participate in public affairs. More elections are held than ever before throughout the world. Yet these processes at times occur in the context of a deterioration of democracy and increasing threats to civic space. With the digitalization of electoral processes, new human rights challenges have arisen from the use of information and communications technology (ICT), such as disinformation online, especially through social media. It is therefore essential to bear in mind the centrality of respect for human rights and fundamental freedoms in free and genuine elections.

2. Participation in public affairs, including through elections, is a human right protected by international human rights law instruments. It is guaranteed by the Universal Declaration of Human Rights and subsequent treaty provisions, notably article 25 of the International Covenant on Civil and Political Rights (see annex I). At the regional level, the African, Inter-American and European human rights systems have also recognized this fundamental right (see annex II). Countries and people across the globe have recognized that free and genuine elections are a crucial democratic requirement and an imperative means of giving voice to the will of the people, which is the basis of government authority.

3. Besides participation being a human right in itself, other human rights are central to electoral processes. For the right to vote and be elected to be exercised meaningfully, it is important that there is an environment in which human rights are respected and enjoyed by all individuals, in particular the rights to equality and non-discrimination, to freedom of opinion and expression, to freedom of peaceful assembly and association, to security and to an effective remedy.

4. The present handbook comprehensively outlines universal human rights norms and standards applicable in the context of elections. Over the years, the United Nations has elaborated international norms and standards relating to elections and political participation. Human rights expert mechanisms, in particular treaty bodies and the special procedures of the Human Rights Council, have interpreted the norms and standards enshrined in the relevant international instruments through their monitoring, decisions and recommendations. This has helped clarify human rights norms and standards applicable to electoral processes. This evolving body of interpretations and recommendations provides guidance on how human rights mechanisms and bodies understand norms and

standards to apply in specific contexts. Annex III provides information on the nature and mandate of the United Nations human rights mechanisms and the legal nature of their interpretations and recommendations.

5. While acknowledging the development of relevant standards by regional human rights systems (see annex II), the handbook focuses on universal norms and standards and therefore on the contribution of the United Nations to international human rights law relating to elections and political participation.

6. The handbook aims at raising awareness and building technical capacity on human rights issues that arise in electoral contexts. It also intends to provide guidance to policymakers and government officials on the human rights obligations of States in the context of elections and to support the development of effective legal frameworks for the exercise of electoral rights.

7. The handbook was prepared by the Office of the United Nations High Commissioner for Human Rights (OHCHR) and has benefited from review and comments by partners in the electoral field. The first chapter describes how OHCHR supports States in implementing relevant international human rights norms and standards relevant to the legal and technical aspects of electoral processes. Chapter II outlines United Nations human rights norms and standards relating to electoral processes in general, while chapter III reviews the relevant criteria in detail. Finally, chapter IV explores other human rights considerations that should be taken into account when designing and implementing electoral legal frameworks.

I. INVOLVEMENT OF THE OFFICE OF THE UNITED NATIONS HIGH COMMISSIONER FOR HUMAN RIGHTS IN ELECTORAL PROCESSES

8. United Nations engagement with Member States in electoral processes is founded on human rights norms and standards guaranteeing political participation.[1] Human rights work in the context of electoral processes is thus essential during all phases (before, during and after election day(s)) to uphold a safe and peaceful environment and to strengthen the credibility of such processes.

9. While elections provide people with opportunities to freely express their will and exercise their civil and political rights, especially the right to participate in public affairs, these events may also exacerbate existing tensions and the risk of human rights violations and abuses. Some rights may be threatened in the context of elections, particularly freedoms of opinion and expression, peaceful assembly and association, and the right to participate in public affairs. Electoral processes may also sometimes trigger arbitrary arrests and detention, ill-treatment and torture, extrajudicial killings, disappearances and other human rights violations. Violations of economic, social and cultural rights can also give rise to tensions in the context of elections.

10. Some individuals and groups may also risk being subjected to violence or suffer discrimination when exercising their rights. Depending on the context, these may include persons who regularly and visibly engage in public debate on critical issues, including human rights, good governance and corruption, such as members of the opposition and political activists, human rights defenders, representatives of non-governmental organizations (NGOs), journalists and media workers, but also specific groups that are commonly victims of discrimination and violence, namely women, young persons, lesbian, gay, bisexual, transgender and intersex persons, minorities, indigenous peoples, persons with disabilities, refugees and asylum seekers, internally displaced persons, stateless persons and migrants. Women, who are represented in most of the above groups, will often be particularly at risk.

11. Human rights work is important in the context of all electoral processes, such as presidential and legislative elections, major referendums (e.g. on constitutions or on secession) and local, regional and territorial elections, especially in situations in which the risk of violence and human rights violations and abuses is high.

---

1 A/72/260, para. 27.

12. Before an election, it is important to ensure that the relevant legal framework (e.g. the Constitution, electoral law, legislation on political parties, and procedure (party registration, candidates' vetting, voter registration, out-of-country voting, etc.)) complies with the State's obligations under international human rights law and that the relevant institutions (e.g. election management body, media commission and courts) can function independently and/or impartially. During the pre-polling and polling phases, it is critical for the authorities to ensure a safe and enabling environment that is conducive to safely and freely exercising the right to participate in public affairs. Prerequisite rights should be upheld, including the rights to freedom of opinion and expression, peaceful assembly and association, and movement, but also freedom from discrimination and violence, the right to a fair trial and an effective remedy, and the right to education. Electoral processes reveal the dynamics between Government and civil society. Restrictions on fundamental freedoms tend to be a crucial factor in the escalation of tension. The post-election period may also be sensitive as results may be contested. Therefore, it is essential for public authorities to ensure a conducive environment for participation and respect for prerequisite human rights. They should also ensure that any violations or abuses of human rights are promptly and impartially investigated and that those responsible are held accountable.

13. In accordance with the mandate of the United Nations High Commissioner for Human Rights to promote and protect all human rights of all people everywhere,[2] OHCHR can engage in comprehensive human rights work and thus play a significant role throughout the various phases of the electoral cycle (pre-polling, polling and/or post-polling).[3] In particular, OHCHR, alongside other United Nations partners, can help foster an environment conducive to inclusive and peaceful elections and respect for relevant human rights standards[4] through a wide range of activities. This supports broader United Nations efforts to assist Member States, where appropriate and upon request, in creating a conducive environment for holding peaceful and credible elections through good offices, support for political dialogue, facilitation and mediation, often in collaboration with regional and subregional entities or other actors.

---

2 See General Assembly resolution 48/141.

3 In several resolutions, the General Assembly has requested the Secretary-General to continue to ensure that OHCHR is able to respond, within its mandate and in close coordination with the Electoral Assistance Division, to the numerous and increasingly complex and comprehensive requests from Member States for advisory services. See, most recently, General Assembly resolution 74/158, para. 17.

4 Department of Political and Peacebuilding Affairs, "Policy on principles and types of UN electoral assistance" (2021).

14. Such OHCHR activities include:

(a) Monitoring, particularly for early warning and prevention purposes, in situations in which there are concerns about potential violence and human rights violations, especially concerning groups in vulnerable situations;

(b) Supporting and organizing advocacy for peaceful elections, electoral laws and institutions that are compliant with human rights, thus allowing for the full participation of the electorate;

(c) Reporting on human rights violations before, during and after election day, particularly on violations of the rights to freedom of opinion and expression, peaceful assembly and association, and to be free from violence, including sexual violence, ill-treatment and torture, which can be at risk in the run-up to elections or in the event of post-electoral protests;

(d) Conducting, supporting or participating in investigations or fact-finding missions when serious election-related incidents occur, with a view to ensuring accountability and preventing reoccurrence;[5]

(e) Ensuring protection, especially in the most volatile contexts, with a focus on the sections of the population that are in the most vulnerable situations;

(f) Providing technical assistance and advice, including during the pre-polling period, for instance on ensuring the conformity of the relevant legislation with international human rights standards, and on peace and transitional justice processes, constitution-making, institution-building etc.;

(g) Raising awareness of the centrality of gender equality and the participation of minorities, indigenous peoples and persons with disabilities in the exercise of democratic participation rights and supporting civic convening and other actions aiming at genuine participation by potentially excluded or at-risk populations;

(h) Supporting human rights mechanisms, including treaty bodies and special procedure mandate holders, including by assisting, as relevant, the engagement of special procedure mandate holders in promoting and protecting human rights in the context of electoral processes.

---

5 OHCHR supports commissions of inquiry and fact-finding missions established by the Human Rights Council, the Security Council or the Secretary-General, often acting as their secretariat. In accordance with the mandate of the High Commissioner, mechanisms can also be set up to look into violations of human rights in the context of electoral processes, for example the OHCHR fact-finding mission to Kenya in 2008. See OHCHR, "Report from OHCHR fact-finding mission to Kenya, 6–28 February 2008".

15. OHCHR engagement may vary depending on whether it is present in the field. In situations in which it is present in the field, OHCHR is particularly well placed to engage in the context of electoral processes, especially where violence and/or human rights violations can be anticipated or emerge unexpectedly. Where OHCHR is not present in the field and the political and social situation seems unstable, it can deploy rapid response missions, either independently or to support or participate in initiatives led by other United Nations entities. System-wide coherence and cooperation among all United Nations entities involved in supporting in-country electoral activities is crucial to ensure that such efforts are provided in a complementary manner, avoiding duplication and ensuring that the United Nations delivers as one.

United Nations electoral assistance

The framework for United Nations electoral assistance was established by the General Assembly in 1991. Since then, United Nations electoral assistance has evolved to respond to the changing needs of Member States seeking to conduct free and genuine elections.

In order to ensure coherence and consistency in the United Nations' provision of electoral assistance through various complementary entities,[6] in 1991, pursuant to General Assembly resolution 46/137, the Secretary-General designated the Under-Secretary-General for Political Affairs as the focal point for electoral assistance across the United Nations system. The focal point plays a leadership role and is responsible for setting electoral assistance policies, deciding on the parameters of United Nations electoral assistance and maintaining a single electoral roster of experts. With the restructuring of the United Nations peace and security pillar, the Under-Secretary-General for Political and Peacebuilding Affairs serves as the focal point and is supported by the Electoral Assistance Division of the Department of Political and Peacebuilding Affairs of the Secretariat. The Electoral Assistance Division provides political and technical guidance to all United Nations entities engaged in electoral assistance, including on policies and good practices.

---

6 United Nations entities providing electoral assistance include the Department of Political and Peacebuilding Affairs, the Department of Peace Operations, the United Nations Development Programme (UNDP), OHCHR, United Nations Volunteers, the United Nations Educational, Scientific and Cultural Organization, the United Nations Entity for Gender Equality and the Empowerment of Women (UN-Women) and the International Organization for Migration. See also https://dppa.un.org/en/elections.

United Nations electoral assistance is provided only at the specific request of a Member State or on the basis of a mandate from the Security Council or the General Assembly. The General Assembly has repeatedly highlighted that United Nations assistance should be guided by such key principles as objectivity, impartiality, neutrality and independence, with due respect for national sovereignty. United Nations electoral assistance is also expected to always promote the participation, representation and empowerment of women and marginalized groups in electoral processes.

Demand for electoral assistance remains high. Since 1991, more than 100 countries have requested and received United Nations electoral assistance, including in some of the most challenging post-conflict and geographical environments.[7] Technical assistance is the most frequent form of electoral assistance provided. The United Nations may also assist Member States in creating an environment conducive to holding peaceful and credible elections through good offices, support for political dialogue, facilitation and mediation. United Nations electoral assistance, such as supervision, observation, panels and certification, requires a mandate by the Security Council or the General Assembly. Support may also be provided to international observers, although this occurs only rarely. The Inter-Agency Coordination Mechanism for United Nations Electoral Assistance, convened and chaired by the Electoral Assistance Division, serves as the platform for information exchange, coordination and the development of internal policies among members of the United Nations system, including OHCHR, involved in electoral matters.

The General Assembly regularly requests OHCHR to continue to respond, within its mandate and in close coordination with the Electoral Assistance Division, to the numerous and increasingly complex and comprehensive requests from Member States for advisory services.[8] The present handbook is intended, among other things, to enhance the ability of OHCHR and the United Nations system as a whole to support States in promoting and protecting human rights in the context of electoral processes.

[7] See https://dppa.un.org/en/elections.
[8] General Assembly resolution 74/158, para. 17.

II. INTERNATIONAL HUMAN RIGHTS STANDARDS REGARDING ELECTORAL PROCESSES IN GENERAL

A. Basic norms and standards regarding elections and political participation

16. The basic universal norms and standards[9] relating to elections and political participation are as follows:

Universal Declaration of Human Rights

Article 21

1. Everyone has the right to take part in the government of his country, directly or through freely chosen representatives.
2. Everyone has the right of equal access to public service in his country.
3. The will of the people shall be the basis of the authority of government; this will shall be expressed in periodic and genuine elections which shall be by universal and equal suffrage and shall be held by secret vote or by equivalent free voting procedures.

International Covenant on Civil and Political Rights

Article 25

Every citizen shall have the right and the opportunity, without any of the distinctions mentioned in article 2 and without unreasonable restrictions:

(a) To take part in the conduct of public affairs, directly or through freely chosen representatives;

(b) To vote and to be elected at genuine periodic elections which shall be by universal and equal suffrage and shall be held by secret ballot, guaranteeing the free expression of the will of the electors;

(c) To have access, on general terms of equality, to public service in his country.

[9] For relevant regional standards, see annex II.

17. International norms and standards on political participation involve three central rights: the right to take part in the conduct of public affairs; the right to vote and to be elected; and the right to have access to public service. The Human Rights Committee has defined the conduct of public affairs as "a broad concept which relates to the exercise of political power, in particular the exercise of legislative, executive and administrative powers. It covers all aspects of public administration, and the formulation and implementation of policy at international, national, regional and local levels".[10]

18. Furthermore, the Universal Declaration of Human Rights states that the will of the people shall be the basis of the authority of government. Human rights and democracy are closely linked.[11] Likewise, respect for human rights is essential for the will of the people to be respected in electoral processes. As stated by the Human Rights Committee, "article 25 lies at the core of democratic government based on the consent of the people".[12] More specifically, "elections lie at the heart of democracy, and remain the primary means through which individuals exercise their right to participate in public affairs."[13]

19. Participation rights may only be subject to limitations that are established by law, are non-discriminatory and are based on objective and reasonable criteria.[14] The Human Rights Committee has clarified these criteria in its general comment No. 25 (1996). The right to vote may be subject only to reasonable restrictions, such as setting a minimum age limit.[15] On the other hand, certain limitations on the right to vote constitute discrimination. Participatory rights are not to be unduly limited on the basis of race, colour, sex, language, religion, political or other opinion, national or social origin, property, birth, disability or other status. Discriminatory limitations include but are not limited to economic requirements,

---

[10] Human Rights Committee, general comment No. 25 (1996), para. 5.

[11] Human Rights Council resolution 19/36, para. 4, in which the Council stated that democracy was vital for the promotion and protection of all human rights.

[12] Human Rights Committee, general comment No. 25 (1996), para. 1.

[13] Guidelines for States on the effective implementation of the right to participate in public affairs (A/HRC/39/28), para. 25.

[14] Human Rights Committee, general comment No. 25 (1996), paras. 3–4. See also, inter alia, *Staderini and De Lucia v. Italy* (CCPR/C/127/D/2656/2015), para. 9.5; *Delgado Burgoa v. Plurinational State of Bolivia* (CCPR/C/122/D/2628/2015), para. 11.5; *Nasheed v. Maldives* (CCPR/C/122/D/2270/2013-CCPR/C/122/D/2851/2016), para. 8.6; and *Paksas v. Lithuania* (CCPR/C/110/D/2155/2012), para. 8.4.

[15] Human Rights Committee, general comment No. 25 (1996), para. 10.

such as those based on ownership of property;[16] excessive residency requirements;[17] restrictions on the right to vote for naturalized citizens (as opposed to citizens by birth);[18] literacy or educational requirements;[19] and excessive restrictions on the voting rights of convicted prisoners.[20] Regarding the right to stand for elections, any restriction, such as a minimum age, must also be justifiable on objective and reasonable criteria. Unreasonable or discriminatory requirements include language, education, overly strict residency criteria, descent and political affiliation,[21] such as the failure or refusal to register candidates because they belong to a political opposition group.[22] Additionally, restrictions on political participation on the grounds of disability are considered as discriminatory under the Convention on the Rights of Persons with Disabilities, as outlined below.[23]

20. Similar to the right to vote and the right to stand for election, the right of equal access to public service[24] is expressly subject to the prohibition of discrimination under article 2 of the International Covenant on Civil and Political Rights. The Covenant allows certain requirements to access public service, but the criteria

---

16 Ibid., para. 3.

17 Ibid., para. 10. See also CCPR/C/UZB/CO/4, para. 26.

18 Human Rights Committee, general comment No. 25 (1996), para. 3. See also CCPR/C/KWT/CO/3, paras. 46–47.

19 Human Rights Committee, general comment No. 25 (1996), para. 10.

20 Ibid., para. 14. See also *Yevdokimov and Rezanov v. Russian Federation* (CCPR/C/101/D/1410/2005), para. 7.5; CCPR/C/EST/CO/4, paras. 33–34; CCPR/C/TKM/CO/2, paras. 50–51; CCPR/C/GBR/CO/7, para. 25; and CCPR/C/KHM/CO/2, para. 26. See also guidelines for States on the effective implementation of the right to participate in public affairs, para. 42.

21 Human Rights Committee, general comment No. 25 (1996), para. 15. See also CCPR/C/TJK/CO/3, paras. 54–55 (a).

22 *Sudalenko v. Belarus* (CCPR/C/100/D/1354/2005), paras. 6.6–6.7.

23 Convention on the Rights of Persons with Disabilities, arts. 2, 5 (2) and 29. Disability-based discrimination is defined in article 2 as "any distinction, exclusion or restriction on the basis of disability which has the purpose or effect of impairing or nullifying the recognition, enjoyment or exercise, on an equal basis with others, of all human rights and fundamental freedoms in the political, economic, social, cultural, civil or any other field. It includes all forms of discrimination, including denial of reasonable accommodation." See also Committee on the Rights of Persons with Disabilities, general comment No. 6 (2018).

24 International Covenant on Civil and Political Rights, art. 25 (c). See also International Convention on the Elimination of All Forms of Racial Discrimination, art. 5; Convention on the Elimination of All Forms of Discrimination against Women, art. 7; and Convention on the Rights of Persons with Disabilities, art. 29.

and processes for appointment, promotion, suspension and dismissal must be transparent, objective and reasonable.[25]

21. Other universal human rights instruments contain relevant provisions, namely the International Covenant on Economic, Social and Cultural Rights (art. 8); the International Convention on the Elimination of All Forms of Racial Discrimination (art. 5 (c)); the Convention on the Elimination of All Forms of Discrimination against Women (arts. 7–8); the Convention on the Rights of the Child (art. 15); the Convention on the Rights of Persons with Disabilities (arts. 3 (c), 4 (3), 29 and 33 (3)); the International Convention on the Protection of All Migrant Workers and Members of Their Families (arts. 41–42); the Declaration on the Rights of Persons Belonging to National or Ethnic, Religious and Linguistic Minorities (art. 2 (2)); the United Nations Declaration on the Rights of Indigenous Peoples (arts. 5 and 18); the Durban Declaration and Programme of Action (para. 32); the Declaration on the Right to Development (arts. 1 (1), 2 and 8 (2)); and the Declaration on the Right and Responsibility of Individuals, Groups and Organs of Society to Promote and Protect Universally Recognized Human Rights and Fundamental Freedoms (art. 8). Annex I to this handbook sets out the texts of the basic international human rights norms and standards relating to elections and political participation.

22. United Nations human rights mechanisms have developed and given authoritative interpretation of those standards in studies, Views on individual complaints or general interpretative documents, such as general comments or recommendations. In particular, the Human Rights Committee has provided its interpretation of article 25 of the International Covenant on Civil and Political Rights in its general comment No. 25 (1996) on the right to participate in public affairs, voting rights and the right of equal access to public service.[26] In this important document, the Human Rights Committee clarifies the scope of the rights guaranteed in article 25 of the Covenant.[27]

---

25 Human Rights Committee, general comment No. 25 (1996), para. 23. See also *Bandaranayake v. Sri Lanka* (CCPR/C/93/D/1376/2005), para. 7.1; and *Sudalenko v. Belarus*, para. 6.4. See also *L.G. v. Republic of Korea* (CERD/C/86/D/51/2012), para. 7.4, on mandatory HIV/AIDS and drug tests required from foreign teachers of English.

26 Human Rights Committee, general comment No. 25 (1996). See also Committee on the Elimination of Discrimination against Women, general recommendation No. 23 (1997); and Committee on the Rights of Persons with Disabilities, general comment No. 7 (2018).

27 Please refer to annex III for additional information on the jurisprudence of human rights treaty bodies.

23. In 2018, the Human Rights Council, in its resolution 39/11, presented the guidelines for States on the effective implementation of the right to participate in public affairs as a set of orientations for States, as well as for, where appropriate, other relevant stakeholders in relation to the effective implementation of the right to participate in public affairs. The guidelines constitute a useful tool for States as they refer to basic principles underpinning the effective implementation of this right and provide practical recommendations concerning the right to participate in electoral processes.

B. Non-discrimination

24. The Universal Declaration of Human Rights (art. 2), the International Covenant on Civil and Political Rights (art. 2 (1)) and the International Covenant on Economic, Social and Cultural Rights (art. 2 (2)) provide that the enjoyment of the rights contained therein shall be without any discrimination of any kind as to race, colour, sex, language, religion, political or other opinion, national or social origin, property, birth or other status. Furthermore, the Convention on the Elimination of All Forms of Discrimination against Women (arts. 1–2) provides for additional protection for women against all forms of discrimination.

25. To ensure the inclusion of groups that historically have been and continue to be disenfranchised, other international instruments specifically guarantee the equal enjoyment of participation rights by persons with disabilities, members of minority groups and indigenous peoples.[28]

C. Self-determination

26. The notion of democratic elections may be said to be rooted in the fundamental principle of self-determination. Participatory rights under article 25 of the International Covenant on Civil and Political Rights are related to, but distinct from, the right of peoples to self-determination. The right to self-determination is recognized in the Charter of the United Nations (Article 1 (2)) and in article 1 common to the International Covenant on Civil and Political Rights and the International Covenant on Economic, Social and Cultural Rights.[29] The Human Rights Committee has emphasized that articles 25 and 27 (relating to minority rights) of the International Covenant on Civil and Political Rights

---

[28] Convention on the Rights of Persons with Disabilities, art. 29; and International Convention on the Elimination of Racial Discrimination, art. 5 (c). See annex I.

[29] See Human Rights Committee, general comment No. 12 (1984).

are distinct from article 1.[30] The Charter further emphasizes the importance of self-determination in regard to non-self-governing and trust territories (Articles 73 (2) and 76 (2)). The right to self-determination has two aspects, namely external and internal, depending on the circumstances. External self-determination refers to the right of peoples to be independent and determine their own political status, while internal self-determination concerns the right of peoples within a State to govern themselves without outside interference. Peoples first need to be independent and freely determine their political status (International Covenant on Civil and Political Rights, art. 1). Once they are constituted as a state or a community within a State, they are able to freely choose their representatives and exercise their participatory rights (ibid., art. 25). Accordingly, the Human Rights Committee has interpreted article 25 in the light of article 1.[31]

D. Prerequisite rights

27. An enabling human rights environment is also essential to ensure free and genuine elections. The prevailing atmosphere should be one of respect for human rights and fundamental freedoms. A number of fundamental rights and freedoms take on additional importance in the context of electoral processes, such as freedom of opinion and expression, including the right of access to information, freedom of peaceful assembly, freedom of association, freedom from discrimination and equal access to participation, freedom of movement, as well as the right to security of person, the right to a fair trial and an effective remedy and the right to education. These prerequisite rights are addressed in chapter III below.

---

30 Human Rights Committee, general comment No. 25 (1996), para. 2, and general comment No. 23 (1994), para. 3.1.

31 The Human Rights Committee has interpreted the right of political participation of indigenous peoples in the light of the right to self-determination. See *Sanila-Aikio v. Finland* (CCPR/C/124/D/2668/2015), para. 6.11, regarding the right to political participation of the Sami people, in which the Committee found "a violation of the author's rights under article 25 [of the International Covenant on Civil and Political Rights], read alone and in conjunction with article 27, as interpreted in the light of article 1 of the Covenant".

III. INTERNATIONAL CRITERIA REVIEWED IN DETAIL

28. International human rights norms and standards contain a number of fundamental criteria for free and genuine elections. In the present chapter those criteria are reviewed in detail.

A. Free elections

1. Essence of free elections: the will of the people

29. The ultimate indication of whether elections are "free" is the extent to which they allow for the full expression of the political will of the people concerned. According to the Universal Declaration of Human Rights (art. 21 (3)), it is the will of the people that is the very basis of legitimate governmental authority. The Universal Declaration of Human Rights also provides that everyone has the right to take part in the government of their country, directly or through freely chosen representatives (art. 21 (1)). This right is echoed in a similar provision in article 25 (a) of the International Covenant on Civil and Political Rights. The Human Rights Committee considers that this provision "lies at the core of democratic government based on the consent of the people"[32] and has indicated that any electoral system must guarantee and give effect to the free expression of the will of the electors.[33] The Convention on the Rights of Persons with Disabilities also guarantees the right of persons with disabilities to political participation, on an equal basis with others (art. 29 (a)), and the free expression of the will of persons with disabilities as electors (art. 29 (a) (iii)).

30. Furthermore, the International Covenant on Civil and Political Rights and the International Covenant on Economic, Social and Cultural Rights state that, by virtue of their right to self-determination, all people have the right to freely determine their political status (common art. 1). The Charter of the United Nations reflects identical concerns, particularly in regard to non-self-governing and trust territories. The Charter mandates assistance to peoples in non-self-governing territories in the development of free political institutions (Article 73 (2)).

---

32 Human Rights Committee, general comment No. 25 (1996), para. 1.

33 CCPR/C/LAO/CO/1, para. 37. See also CCPR/CO/79/GNQ, para. 12.

2. Prerequisite rights

31. To be free, participation in the electoral process requires a safe environment in which all human rights are fully respected and enjoyed by all individuals.[34] To that end, obstacles to full participation must be removed and all individuals must be confident that no personal harm will befall them or their relatives or colleagues as a result of their participation. Of particular relevance in this context are the rights addressed below.

(a) Non-discrimination and equal access to participation

32. The right to equality and non-discrimination must be respected so that all citizens are ensured equal access to participation in electoral processes. The right to freedom from discrimination is guaranteed by articles 2 and 7 of the Universal Declaration of Human Rights and is further defined by articles 2 (1), 3 and 26 of the International Covenant on Civil and Political Rights:

International Covenant on Civil and Political Rights

Article 2

1. Each State Party to the present Covenant undertakes to respect and to ensure to all individuals within its territory and subject to its jurisdiction the rights recognized in the present Covenant, without distinction of any kind, such as race, colour, sex, language, religion, political or other opinion, national or social origin, property, birth or other status.

. . .

Article 3

The States Parties to the present Covenant undertake to ensure the equal right of men and women to the enjoyment of all civil and political rights set forth in the present Covenant.

Article 26

All persons are equal before the law and are entitled without any discrimination to the equal protection of the law. In this respect, the law shall prohibit any discrimination and guarantee to all persons equal and effective protection against discrimination on any ground such as race, colour, sex, language, religion, political or other opinion, national or social origin, property, birth or other status.

---

[34] See guidelines for States on the effective implementation of the right to participate in public affairs, and the corresponding recommendations.

33. Under article 26 of the International Covenant on Civil and Political Rights, States have both a positive legal obligation to prevent discrimination and a negative obligation to refrain from discriminating. In addition, article 26 requires equal protection under the law in all areas in which a State party legislates.

34. Other treaty provisions also guarantee non-discrimination and equal participation in public affairs in relation to various groups, imposing both negative and positive obligations. The International Convention on the Elimination of All Forms of Racial Discrimination prohibits any racial discrimination (art. 5 (c)), while the International Convention on the Suppression and Punishment of the Crime of Apartheid prohibits legislative and other measures calculated to prevent racial groups from participating in the political life of the country (art. II (c)). The Convention on the Elimination of All Forms of Discrimination against Women prohibits discrimination based on sex (art. 2) and guarantees equal access to participation for women (art. 7). Other international human rights law instruments guarantee equal access to participation for persons with disabilities (Convention on the Rights of Persons with Disabilities, art. 29) and children who are capable of forming their own views (Convention on the Rights of the Child, art. 12, and Convention on the Rights of Persons with Disabilities, art. 7 (3)). In situations in which there are linguistic minorities, the Human Rights Committee has stated that information and materials about voting should be available in minority languages.[35]

35. During an election period, the importance of an atmosphere free from discrimination cannot be overstated. An environment in which discrimination is tolerated facilitates intimidation and manipulation of the electorate, thereby undermining opportunities for free elections. The application of international norms and standards on equality and non-discrimination is essential to permit and facilitate political participation, thereby guaranteeing genuine choice for voters and the right of candidates to stand for election. Furthermore, international human rights law standards guarantee the rights of all other actors involved in elections, such as voters, activists and civil society. Accordingly, all persons must be afforded equal access to all electoral events and all candidates must be granted fair media access for campaigning and advertising purposes.[36]

---

[35] Human Rights Committee, general comment No. 25 (1996), para. 12.

[36] See section I of chapter IV below regarding fair media access by all political candidates and parties. See also A/HRC/26/30, para. 48.

36. Effective participation in public and political life can be unduly limited or prevented by formal and substantive discrimination on any of the grounds listed in article 2 of the International Covenant on Civil and Political Rights. The category of "other status" is non-exhaustive and has been interpreted by human rights mechanisms as including discrimination on the grounds of age, gender identity, disability, nationality and sexual orientation. For example, human rights mechanisms have noted that criminal law sanctions that target lesbian, gay, bisexual, transgender and intersex persons, as well as discriminatory restrictions on their freedoms of peaceful assembly, association and expression, result in severe limitations on their participation in political and public life.[37]

(b) Freedom of opinion and expression

37. The rights to freedom of opinion and expression are protected by article 19 of the Universal Declaration of Human Rights and article 19 of the International Covenant on Civil and Political Rights,[38] which reads:

International Covenant on Civil and Political Rights

Article 19

1. Everyone shall have the right to hold opinions without interference.
2. Everyone shall have the right to freedom of expression; this right shall include freedom to seek, receive and impart information and ideas of all kinds, regardless of frontiers, either orally, in writing or in print, in the form of art, or through any other media of his choice.
3. The exercise of the rights provided for in paragraph 2 of this article carries with it special duties and responsibilities. It may therefore be subject to certain restrictions, but these shall only be such as are provided by law and are necessary:

   (a) For respect of the rights or reputations of others;

   (b) For the protection of national security or of public order (*ordre public*), or of public health or morals.

---

37 A/HRC/27/29, para. 43.

38 See also International Convention on the Elimination of All Forms of Racial Discrimination, art. 5 (d) (viii); International Covenant on Economic, Social and Cultural Rights, art. 15 (3); International Convention on the Protection of the Rights of All Migrant Workers and Members of Their Families, art. 13 (1); and Convention on the Rights of Persons with Disabilities, art. 21.

38. Under the International Covenant on Civil and Political Rights, the right to freedom of opinion is guaranteed "without interference". Unlike freedom of expression and information, this right is absolute and cannot be restricted or interfered with in any manner.[39] Freedom of opinion extends to the right to change an opinion whenever and for whatever reason a person so freely chooses and necessarily includes freedom not to express one's opinion.[40] The unconditional freedom to hold a political opinion is imperative in the context of electoral processes since the authentic assertion of popular will is impossible in an environment in which such freedom is absent or restricted in any way

39. The right to freedom of expression is guaranteed in article 19 (2) of the International Covenant on Civil and Political Rights.41 In terms of content, this right includes the freedom to seek, receive and impart information and ideas of all kinds. In its general comment No. 25 (1996), the Human Rights Committee has stated that "in order to ensure the full enjoyment of rights protected by article 25, the free communication of information and ideas about public and political issues between citizens, candidates and elected representatives is essential. This implies a free press and other media able to comment on public issues without censorship or restraint and to inform public opinion."42 Furthermore, the scope of the provision is not confined to one medium of expression, but includes, among others, cultural, artistic and other forms of expression, including speech, books, newspapers, pamphlets, posters, banners, dress, legal submissions and the Internet.[43]

40. In conjunction with article 19 of the International Covenant on Civil and Political Rights, article 25 thereof secures the right of access to information, including the right of the media to access information on public affairs and

---

39 Human Rights Committee, general comment No. 34 (2011), paras. 5 and 9.

40 Ibid., paras. 9–10. See also *Park v. Republic of Korea* (CCPR/C/64/D/628/1995) (convicted and sentenced for having opinions critical of the Government); Human Rights Committee, *Kang v. Republic of Korea*, communication No. 878/99, paras. 7.2 and 8 (person held in solitary confinement for 13 years for holding communist political opinions and subjected to "ideology conversion").

41 The right to freedom of expression is also guaranteed by other treaty provisions, namely: International Convention on the Elimination of All Forms of Racial Discrimination, art. 5 (d) (viii); International Covenant on Economic, Social and Cultural Rights, art. 15 (3); Convention on the Rights of the Child, arts. 12–13; International Convention on the Protection of the Rights of All Migrant Workers and Members of Their Families art. 13; and Convention on the Rights of Persons with Disabilities, art. 21.

42 Human Rights Committee, general comment No. 25 (1996), para. 25. See also general comment No. 34 (2011), para. 13.

43 Human Rights Committee, general comment No. 34 (2011), para. 12.

the right of the general public to receive media output.[44] To give effect to the right of access to information, States parties should proactively put in the public domain government information of public interest. States parties should make every effort to ensure easy, prompt, effective and practical access to such information.[45]

41. An electoral process is the expression of the political will of the people. The right to express diverse ideas must, therefore, be firmly guarded during election periods. More precisely, in the context of elections and political communications, dedicated attention is to be afforded to the rights to free expression of the main actors: the voters, who depend on the right to freedom of expression to receive full and accurate information, and express their political affiliation without fear; candidates and political organizations, who need to exercise their rights through campaigning and communicating their political messages freely without interference or attacks; and the media and civil society organizations, which rely on the right to freedom of expression to play their essential democratic role of informing the public, scrutinizing political parties and platforms, and providing checks and balances in the electoral process.[46]

42. However, the right to freedom of expression may be subject to certain limitations in accordance with article 19 (3) of the International Covenant on Civil and Political Rights. Any restrictions must be prescribed by law and necessary for a legitimate purpose, namely to protect the rights or reputation of others, national security, public order or public health and morals. In other words, the limitations were not included in article 19 (3) to provide States with an excuse for placing restrictions on free expression. In reviewing such cases, the Human Rights Committee has held that, while it may be legitimate to restrict freedom of expression in order to protect the right to vote under article 25, such restrictions must not impede political debate. For example, punishing an individual for making calls to boycott a non-compulsory vote would not constitute a permissible limitation on freedom of expression necessary for the respect of the rights of others.[47] With regard to the protection of public morals, any such limitations must be understood in the light of the universality of human rights and

---

[44] Ibid., para. 18, referring to Human Rights Caommittee, *Gauthier v. Canada*, communication No. 633/95, and *Mavlonov and Sa'di v. Uzbekistan* (CCPR/C/95/D/1334/2004).

[45] Human Rights Committee, general comment No. 34 (2011), para. 19.

[46] A/HRC/26/30, para. 11.

[47] Human Rights Committee, general comment No. 34 (2011), para. 28, referring to *Svetik v. Belarus* (CCPR/C/81/D/927/2000), para. 7.3.

the principle of non-discrimination.[48] Regarding laws relating to threats to national security (e.g. treason, sedition, terrorism or disclosure of official secrets), the precise nature of the threat must be specified.[49] More generally, the Human Rights Committee has outlined that, when a State invokes a legitimate ground for restricting freedom of expression, it must demonstrate in specific and individualized fashion the precise nature of the threat, and the necessity and proportionality of the specific action taken, in particular by establishing a direct and immediate connection between the expression and the threat.[50]

43. Regarding freedom of expression on the Internet, any restrictions on the operation of websites, blogs or any other Internet-based information dissemination system must be established by law, necessary and proportionate.[51] To prohibit such systems from publishing material solely on the basis that they may be critical of the Government or the political social system espoused by the Government is not a permissible restriction.[52] Similarly, blanket Internet shutdowns constitute a violation of international human rights law as they are inherently disproportionate.[53]

44. Freedom of expression may also be limited when the activity or expression seeks to destroy other rights recognized in the International Covenant on Civil and Political Rights.[54] For example, States are required to prohibit by law any

---

48 Human Rights Committee, general comment No. 34 (2011), para. 32.

49 Human Rights Committee, *Kim v. Republic of Korea*, communication No. 574/94, paras. 12.4–12.5.

50 Human Rights Committee, general comment No. 34 (2011), para. 35, referring to *Shin v. Republic of Korea* (CCPR/C/80/D/926/2000).

51 Human Rights Committee, general comment No. 34 (2011), para. 22. Restrictions on the right to freedom of expression must conform to the strict tests of legality (they must be provided by law), necessity (they must be necessary in a democratic society) and proportionality (they must be proportionate to the interest to be protected). See also Special Rapporteur on the promotion and protection of the right to freedom of opinion and expression, "Freedom of expression and elections in the digital age", Research Paper 1/2019 (2019), pp. 6–8.

52 Human Rights Committee, general comment No. 34 (2011), para. 43. On blocked access to websites, see CCPR/C/KWT/CO/3, paras. 40–41; CCPR/C/IRN/CO/3, para. 29; and CCPR/CO/84/SYR, para. 13.

53 Human Rights Committee, general comment No. 34 (2011), para. 43. See also Special Rapporteur on the promotion and protection of the right to freedom of opinion and expression of the United Nations, the Representative on Freedom of the Media of the Organization for Security and Cooperation in Europe, the Special Rapporteur for Freedom of Expression of the Organization of American States and the Special Rapporteur on Freedom of Expression and Access to Information of the African Commission on Human and Peoples' Rights, Joint declaration on freedom of expression and responses to conflict situations, 4 May 2015, para. 4 (c).

54 International Covenant on Civil and Political Rights, art. 5 (1).

advocacy of national, racial or religious hatred that constitutes incitement to discrimination, hostility or violence under article 20 (2) of the Covenant.[55] Such restraints are essential at all times, not least during an election period, to ensure that the political environment is free of any forces that may seek to intimidate the electorate or any political actors, or to violate the fundamental rights of any group. However, such restraints should not be used to prevent political opposition from duly exercising their freedom of expression.

45. Freedom of expression of the media is an essential part of the electoral process in keeping the public informed. States have a duty to provide a regulatory environment that facilitates a diverse range of political positions and ensures that voters have access to comprehensive, accurate and reliable information about all aspects of the electoral process.[56] As stated by the Human Rights Committee, the free communication of information and ideas implies a free press and other media able to comment on public issues without censorship or restraint and to inform public opinion.[57] Thus criticism of public figures, including Heads of State and Government, as well as of institutions, such as the army or the administration, should not be prohibited.[58]

46. The requirements of freedom of expression and information obviously have important implications for fair media access and responsible media use.[59] These implications are discussed in section B.6 (Informed choice) and chapter IV, section I (Media: access and regulation), below.

---

55 International Covenant on Civil and Political Rights, art. 20 (2); and International Convention on the Elimination of All Forms of Racial Discrimination, art. 4 (a). See also Committee on the Elimination of Racial Discrimination, general recommendation No. 35 (2013), para. 13; *Rabbae, A.B.S. and N.A. v. Netherlands* (CCPR/C/117/D/2124/2011), para. 10.7; *Faurisson v.* France (CCPR/C/58/D/550/1993), para. 9.6, in which the Committee considered that it was both necessary and proportionate to prohibit the expression of views that raise or strengthen antisemitic feelings; CERD/C/ITA/CO/16-18, para. 17 (dissemination of ideas of racial superiority and incitement to racial hatred); CERD/C/NLD/CO/17-18, para. 8; and A/67/357, para. 34 et seq. See also the Rabat Plan of Action on the prohibition of advocacy of national, racial or religious hatred that constitutes incitement to discrimination, hostility or violence (A/HRC/22/17/Add.4, annex, appendix).

56 A/HRC/26/30, para. 46.

57 Human Rights Committee, general comment No. 25 (1996), para. 25, and general comment No. 34 (2011), para. 13.

58 Human Rights Committee, general comment No. 34 (2011), para. 38. See also *Kankanamge v. Sri Lanka* (CCPR/C/81/D/909/2000), para. 9.4; CCPR/C/THA/CO/2, paras. 35–36 (criminalization of defamation) and 37–38 (criminalization of criticism and dissention regarding the royal family); and CCPR/C/VEN/CO/4, para. 19 (criminalization of defamation or failing to show respect to the President and other senior figures).

59 See also guidelines for States on the effective implementation of the right to participate in public affairs, paras. 19 (f), 33 and 34.

Internet shutdowns and elections[60]

Internet and telecommunications shutdowns involve measures, which may be in violation of human rights law, to intentionally prevent or disrupt access to or dissemination of information online. Shutdowns are key concerns in today's elections. There may be genuine and plausible motives for Internet disruption, for example, the prevention of violence and the protection of lives in the face of imminent danger. Irrespective of any motive, Internet shutdowns impose significant limitations on the means of communication and expression and on fundamental freedoms. These disruptions can have a particularly strong impact on an electoral process when the sharing of information is critical, given the reliance on digital tools as enablers of political participation or platforms for exchanging information and ideas.

Governments typically conduct or order shutdowns, at times through private actors that operate networks or facilitate network traffic. Large-scale attacks on network infrastructure whether committed by State actors or their agents, such as distributed denial-of-service attacks, may also have shutdown effects. While shutdowns are frequently associated with total network outages, they may also arise when access to mobile communications, websites or social media and messaging applications is blocked, throttled or rendered "effectively unusable". Shutdowns may affect towns or regions within a country, an entire country or even multiple countries and may last for periods ranging from hours to months.

Various United Nations human rights mechanisms have expressed the view that blanket shutdowns and generic blocking and filtering of services are considered violations of international human rights law due to a lack of a legal basis or failure to meet necessity and proportionality requirements.[61] Shutdowns ordered covertly or without an obvious legal basis violate the requirement of article 19 (3) of the International Covenant on Civil and Political Rights, namely that restrictions be "provided by law". Shutdowns ordered pursuant to vaguely formulated laws and regulations may also fail to satisfy the legality requirement. Network shutdowns usually fail to meet the standard of necessity specified by article 19 (3) of the Covenant and may never be invoked to justify the suppression of advocacy for democratic rights. However, Governments sometimes impose shutdowns during demonstrations, elections and other events of extraordinary public interest. "Necessity" under the Covenant means that States should demonstrate that shutdowns are necessary

60 Extracted from A/HRC/41/41and A/HRC/35/22. See also A/HRC/44/24.

61 In its general comment No. 37 (2020), para. 34, the Human Rights Committee stated that "States parties must not, for example, block or hinder Internet connectivity in relation to peaceful assemblies."

to achieve their stated purpose, which in fact they often jeopardize. Although their duration and geographical scope may vary, shutdowns are generally considered a disproportionate restriction on human rights.

The Special Rapporteur on the rights to freedom of peaceful assembly and of association has stated that shutdowns may generate a wide variety of harms to human rights, economic activity, public safety and emergency services that may outweigh any purported benefits.[62] In the context of protests, when tensions are at their highest, Internet access is needed to prevent disinformation and dispel rumours, as well as to protect the rights to liberty and personal integrity, by allowing access to emergency help and contact with family and friends. Due to the negative effects on human rights and the increased reliance on shutdowns by Governments, shutdowns have been condemned by a number of international human rights mechanisms.

(c) Freedom of peaceful assembly

47. The right of peaceful assembly is guaranteed by article 20 of the Universal Declaration of Human Rights and article 21 of the International Covenant on Civil and Political Rights,[63] which reads:

International Covenant on Civil and Political Rights

Article 21

The right of peaceful assembly shall be recognized. No restrictions may be placed on the exercise of this right other than those imposed in conformity with the law and which are necessary in a democratic society in the interests of national security or public safety, public order (*ordre public*), the protection of public health or morals or the protection of the rights and freedoms of others.

48. The right of peaceful assembly protects the non-violent gathering of persons for specific purposes, principally expressive ones.[64] Everyone has the right of peaceful assembly: citizens and non-citizens alike. Article 21 of the International

[62] A/HRC/41/41, paras. 51–53.

[63] See also International Convention on the Elimination of All Forms of Racial Discrimination, art. 5 (d) (ix); and Convention on the Rights of the Child, art. 15.

[64] *Poplavny and Sudalenko v. Belarus* (CCPR/C/118/D/2139/2012), para. 8.5; *Sekerko v. Belarus* (CCPR/C/109/D/1851/2008), para. 9.3; and *Kivenmaa v. Finland* (CCPR/C/50/D/412/1990), para. 7.6.

Covenant on Civil and Political Rights protects peaceful assemblies wherever they take place – outdoors, indoors or online, in public or private spaces or a combination thereof.

49. To enjoy the protection of article 21, an assembly must be peaceful. A presumption exists in favour of considering assemblies to be peaceful.[65] An assembly can still be peaceful even if there are isolated acts of violence by some participants.[66] However, an assembly is no longer "peaceful" if there is widespread and serious violence perpetrated by participants.[67]

50. States must not unduly interfere with peaceful assemblies. They must also facilitate assemblies (in other words, make them possible, for example by blocking off the traffic on streets used for marches) and protect participants (including against potentially violent counterdemonstrations).[68]

51. Peaceful assemblies can only be restricted through necessary and proportionate measures that are provided for by law and are taken in pursuit of one of a limited number of accepted grounds, such as public safety.[69] Blanket bans, which are presumptively disproportionate, should be avoided, unless the State can prove that they conform to the test of necessity and proportionality.[70] Any restriction must be content neutral – in other words, the authorities should not treat assemblies differently simply because of what participants are saying or because of the relationship between the organizers and the authorities.[71]

52. To facilitate the exercise of this right, it is important to allow unimpeded access to and use of the Internet, in particular social media, and other ICT, which are essential tools, especially in times of elections, through which the right to freedom of peaceful assembly can be exercised.[72]

53. Freedom of peaceful assembly in the context of electoral processes is key, since public demonstrations and political rallies are an integral part of such processes and provide

---

65 Human Rights Committee, general comment No. 37 (2020), para. 17.

66 Ibid.

67 Ibid. Violence against participants in a peaceful assembly by the authorities, or by members of the public, including counterdemonstrators, does not render the assembly non-peaceful.

68 Human Rights Committee, general comment No. 37 (2020), paras. 23–24.

69 International Covenant on Civil and Political Rights, art. 21.

70 The Special Rapporteur on the rights to freedom of peaceful assembly and of association considers that "blanket bans, which are intrinsically disproportionate and discriminatory, should be prohibited" (A/68/299, para. 25).

71 Human Rights Committee, general comment No. 37 (2020), para. 22.

72 Ibid., para. 34. See also A/HRC/44/24.

an effective mechanism for the public dissemination of political information. The Human Rights Committee has noted that, since political speech enjoys particular protection as a form of expression, it follows that assemblies with a political message should enjoy a heightened level of accommodation and protection.[73] The Special Rapporteur on the rights to freedom of peaceful assembly and of association considers that the threshold for imposing restrictions in the context of elections should be higher than usual, that is the criteria of "necessity in a democratic society" and "proportionality" should be more difficult to meet during elections.[74]

54. The role of journalists, human rights defenders, election monitors and others involved in monitoring or reporting on assemblies is of importance for the full enjoyment of the right of peaceful assembly. Such persons are entitled to protection under the International Covenant on Civil and Political Rights.[75] Even if an assembly is declared unlawful or is dispersed, that does not terminate the right to monitor.[76]

(d) Freedom of association

55. The right to freedom of association with others is guaranteed by article 20 of the Universal Declaration of Human Rights and article 22 of the International Covenant on Civil and Political Rights,[77] which reads:

International Covenant on Civil and Political Rights

Article 22

1. Everyone shall have the right to freedom of association with others, including the right to form and join trade unions for the protection of his interests.

---

73 Human Rights Committee, general comment No. 34 (2011), paras. 34, 37–38 and 42–43. See also CCPR/C/LAO/CO/1, para. 33.

74 A/68/299, para. 25.

75 Human Rights Committee, general comment No. 37 (2020), para. 30; and *Zhagiparov v. Kazakhstan* (CCPR/C/124/D/2441/2014), paras. 13.2–13.5. See also the Declaration on the Right and Responsibility of Individuals, Groups and Organs of Society to Promote and Protect Universally Recognized Human Rights and Fundamental Freedoms.

76 *Zhagiparov v. Kazakhstan*, paras. 13.2–13.5. See also the Declaration on the Right and Responsibility of Individuals, Groups and Organs of Society to Promote and Protect Universally Recognized Human Rights and Fundamental Freedoms.

77 See also International Convention on the Elimination of All Forms of Racial Discrimination, art. 5 (d) (ix); Convention on the Elimination of All Forms of Discrimination against Women, arts. 7 (c) and 14 (2) (e); Convention on the Rights of the Child, art. 15; International Convention on the Protection of the Rights of All Migrant Workers and Members of Their Families, arts. 26, 40 and 42; International Convention for the Protection of All Persons from Enforced Disappearance, art. 24 (7); and Convention on the Rights of Persons with Disabilities, art. 29 (b) (i).

2. No restrictions may be placed on the exercise of this right other than those which are prescribed by law and which are necessary in a democratic society in the interests of national security or public safety, public order (*ordre public*), the protection of public health or morals or the protection of the rights and freedoms of others. This article shall not prevent the imposition of lawful restrictions on members of the armed forces and of the police in their exercise of this right.
3. Nothing in this article shall authorize States Parties to the International Labour Organisation Convention of 1948 concerning Freedom of Association and Protection of the Right to Organize to take legislative measures which would prejudice, or to apply the law in such a manner as to prejudice, the guarantees provided for in that Convention.

56. The right to freedom of association has a broad scope and includes the right to form and participate in political parties as specific kinds of associations through which individuals can take part in the conduct of political affairs through chosen representatives.[78] Conversely, no one should be compelled to belong to a political party.[79] The right to freedom of association is very closely related to the right to freedom of assembly recognized in article 21 of the Covenant. Accordingly, article 22 (2) permits the same categories of limitations as do articles 19 and 21 (national security, public safety, public order (*ordre public*), the protection of public health or morals or the protection of the rights and freedoms of others). Article 22 also requires procedural safeguards similar to those required in article 21, namely that any restrictions be prescribed by law and be necessary in a democratic society for the protection of public interests. In addition, the scope of article 22 is limited by article 5, which means that the right to freedom of association cannot be interpreted as including any activity that would infringe upon any of the rights protected by the Covenant.

[78] A/68/299, para. 9.
[79] Ibid., para. 30.

57. As with the right to freedom of assembly, it is essential that the right to freedom of association be respected, since the ability to form and join political parties is one of the most important means by which people can participate in the democratic process. The Human Rights Committee has stated that political parties and membership of parties play a significant role in the conduct of public affairs and the electoral process.[80] Thus, their proper functioning should be guaranteed, free from unnecessary interference, while any limitations on their establishment should be construed narrowly and in accordance with the principles of legality, necessity and proportionality.[81]

58. States should ensure that, in their internal management, political parties respect the applicable provisions of article 25 in order to enable citizens to exercise their rights thereunder.[82] To realize women's equal right to participation in public and political life, States must take all appropriate measures to ensure to women the right to form and join associations on equal terms with men,[83] both by abolishing all de jure discrimination and adopting temporary special measures to tackle de facto discrimination.

59. Civil society organizations are inherently different from political parties, the ultimate objective of which is to promote candidates who will run for elections with the aim of governing. In line with this, associations should not be compelled to register as political parties and, conversely, they should not be denied registration as associations because they carry out what the authorities consider to be "political" activities.[84] Freedom of association provides individuals with unique opportunities to express their political opinions, including by holding Governments accountable, through good governance and rule of law initiatives, such as anti-corruption measures, human rights campaigns, institutional reforms and similar measures designed to strengthen democracy.[85]

---

80 Human Rights Committee, general comment No. 25 (1996), para. 26.

81 CCPR/C/TKM/CO/2, para. 49.

82 Human Rights Committee, general comment No. 25 (1996), para. 26.

83 International Covenant on Civil and Political Rights, arts. 2 (1) and 3; International Covenant on Economic, Social and Cultural Rights, art. 2 (2); and Convention on the Elimination of All Forms of Discrimination against Women, art. 7 (c).

84 A/68/299, para. 44.

85 Ibid.

Financing of political parties

The ability of associations, including political parties, to access financial resources is an integral element of the right to freedom of association and has far reaching consequences in the context of elections.[86] Funding ensures that political parties are able to function on a day-to-day basis, to participate in the political arena and to represent a plurality of views, interests and perspectives, thus strengthening democracy.[87] However, funding may also have perverse effects on democratic potential, requiring certain regulation. The Human Rights Committee has noted that reasonable limitations on campaign expenditure may be justified in situations in which this is necessary to ensure that the free choice of voters is not undermined or the democratic process distorted by disproportionate expenditure on behalf of any candidate or party.[88]

The Special Rapporteur on the rights to freedom of peaceful assembly and of association noted that public financing of political parties was often used as an avenue to provide equality of opportunity to all parties, including those that represent marginalized groups, and guarantee competitive participation of diverse ideas and views. Hence, the Special Rapporteur concluded that public funding should not be used to interfere with a party's independence and further or create an overdependency on State resources.[89]

The Special Rapporteur also noted that, more broadly, party resources should be differentiated from public resources. Public resources should not be used to tilt the electoral playing field in favour of a party, in particular the incumbent party or its candidates.[90] This principle extends to the use of State institutions, such as police forces, the judiciary, the prosecutorial authority, law enforcement agencies and others, which should be impartial when controlling or limiting the activities of political parties, such as by initiating politically motivated court cases against rival candidates, preventing them, in effect, from engaging in campaign activities.[91]

---

86 Ibid., para. 34.

87 Ibid.

88 Human Rights Committee, general comment No. 25 (1996), para. 19.

89 A/68/299, para. 35. See also Office for Democratic Institutions and Human Rights (Organization for Security and Cooperation in Europe) and the European Commission for Democracy through Law (Venice Commission), *Guidelines on Political Party Regulation*, 2nd ed. (Strasbourg, 2010), paras. 176–177.

90 A/68/299, para. 36.

91 Ibid.

The Special Rapporteur on the promotion and protection of the right to freedom of opinion and expression noted that political finance was a key concern when protecting and promoting freedom of opinion and expression in electoral and political processes. Restraining campaign spending and creating a level playing field for political parties and candidates are key to ensuring that citizens have access to a diverse range of opinions and political choices. At the same time, the provision of financial support to a political party may in itself be an act of political expression. A careful balance must therefore be struck by each State, reflecting local political values and legal frameworks, while at the same time conforming with international human rights norms. This would require, at a minimum, that States ensure that there is independent monitoring and oversight of political financing, and that every effort is made to ensure that organized crime is prohibited from using campaign financing as a means to gain political influence.[92]

(e) Freedom of movement

60. Freedom of movement is guaranteed by article 13 of the Universal Declaration of Human Rights and article 12 of the International Covenant on Civil and Political Rights,[93] which reads as follows:

International Covenant on Civil and Political Rights

Article 12

1. Everyone lawfully within the territory of a State shall, within that territory, have the right to liberty of movement and freedom to choose his residence.
2. Everyone shall be free to leave any country, including his own.
3. The above-mentioned rights shall not be subject to any restrictions except those which are provided by law, are necessary to protect national security, public order (*ordre public*), public health or morals or the rights and freedoms of others, and are consistent with the other rights recognized in the present Covenant.
4. No one shall be arbitrarily deprived of the right to enter his own country.

---

[92] A/HRC/26/30, para. 65.

[93] See also International Convention on the Elimination of All Forms of Racial Discrimination, art. 5 (d) (i).

61. Freedom of movement is important in electoral processes to ensure that those who are entitled to vote are able to physically access polling stations to exercise that right. It is also indispensable for candidates to carry out their campaigns. This right also allows individuals to participate in electoral processes (e.g. to register to vote, to attend voter information activities etc.) without unlawful, discriminatory or unreasonable restrictions. Article 12 (3) allows the same limitations as those related to the rights to freedom of expression and information, peaceful assembly and association (national security, public safety, public order (*ordre public*), the protection of public health or morals or the protection of the rights and freedoms of others). The Human Rights Committee has clarified that it is not sufficient that the restrictions serve the permissible purposes; they must also be necessary to protect them and proportionate to the interests that they intend to protect.[94] For example, States should not unduly interfere with the activities of opposition political parties by restricting the freedom of movement of their members.[95] States should also take positive measures to overcome impediments to freedom of movement that prevent persons entitled to vote from exercising their rights effectively.[96] This includes ensuring that voting procedures and facilities are accessible to persons with disabilities.[97]

(f) Right to security and freedom from intimidation

62. The Universal Declaration of Human Rights (art. 3) and the International Covenant on Civil and Political Rights (arts. 6 and 9) protect the right to life, liberty and security of person, which may be relevant in electoral contexts when tensions arise.[98] The relevant provisions of the Covenant read as follows:

---

[94] Human Rights Committee, general comment No. 27 (1999), para. 14.
[95] CCPR/CO/80/UGA, para. 22.
[96] Human Rights Committee, general comment No. 25 (1996), para. 12.
[97] Convention on the Rights of Persons with Disabilities, art. 29 (a) (i).
[98] See also Human Rights Committee, general comment No. 35 (2014), para. 9.

International Covenant on Civil and Political Rights

Article 6 (1)

Every human being has the inherent right to life. This right shall be protected by law. No one shall be arbitrarily deprived of his life.

Article 9 (1)

Everyone has the right to liberty and security of person. No one shall be subjected to arbitrary arrest or detention. No one shall be deprived of his liberty except on such grounds and in accordance with such procedure as are established by law.

63. Election-related violence, including sexual violence,[99] may occur during the various phases of an electoral process (i.e. pre-election, on election day(s) or post-election). Human rights defenders, journalists, media workers and other civil society representatives and, in some countries, political activists, in particular members of the opposition, are at greater risk of being victims of human rights violations. As stated by the Special Rapporteur on extrajudicial, summary or arbitrary executions, election-related killings violate not only the right to life, but also the right to participate in the democratic process.[100] Likewise, the Special Rapporteur on violence against women, its causes and consequences has recalled that violence against women in elections remains a major barrier to women's realization of the right to participate in political and public life.[101]

64. The Human Rights Committee has held that any abusive interference with registration or voting, as well as intimidation or coercion of voters, should be prohibited by penal laws and those laws should be strictly enforced.[102] The Committee has also recalled that States parties have an obligation under article 25 of the International Covenant on Civil and Political Rights to ensure the safety

---

[99] See OHCHR, UN-Women and Physicians for Human Rights, "Breaking cycles of violence: gaps in prevention of and response to electoral related sexual violence" (2019).

[100] A/HRC/14/24/Add.7, para. 2. The Special Rapporteur defines "election-related killings" as including "killings: (a) designed to influence, or to prevent attempts to influence, an election outcome; (b) that arise in the context of election processes; or (c) that seek to promote or hinder election-related activity" (ibid., para. 11).

[101] A/73/301, para. 32.

[102] Human Rights Committee, general comment No. 25 (1996), para. 11.

and security of all individuals in the context of elections so that they may exercise their right to vote.[103] For their part, the guidelines for States on the effective implementation of the right to participate in public affairs provide that "States should take measures to protect the safety of candidates, particularly women candidates, who are at risk of violence and intimidation, including gender-based violence, during the electoral process."[104] The Human Rights Committee has requested States to ensure the security and participation of all candidates in elections, including members of opposition parties.[105]

Gender-based violence in the context of elections[106]

Violence against women in electoral contexts remains a major obstacle to the realization of their right to participate in public and political life. Gender-based violence in elections constitutes a human rights violation, prevents women from exercising their political rights and thus negatively affects society as a whole as women are underrepresented at all levels of political decision-making.

While violence against women in politics is not limited to the context of elections, the holding of an election can lead to existing issues being amplified and more visible, the results of which negatively impact women's participation across all aspects of an electoral process, whether as candidates, activists, voters, election officials or journalists. Violence against women in electoral contexts can manifest in different forms throughout the various stages of the process, whether relating to registration and voting, running for elections and political campaigning, the announcement of results and the formation of government. As a result, fewer women may take part in elections as candidates, political campaigners, voters or members of the electoral administration.

Electoral violence has a disproportionate impact on women and differs from that experienced by men. Gender-based violence against women in elections may also consist of threats to their personal security or that of their loved ones. Moreover, women may face violence from their own families and communities. Risks are higher for women of marginalized communities. In some places, harmful cultural and patriarchal norms and discrimination are risk factors

[103] CCPR/C/BGD/CO/1, paras. 29–30.

[104] Para. 37.

[105] CCPR/C/COD/CO/4, para. 48; and CCPR/C/HND/CO/2, para. 45 (a).

[106] See A/73/301. See also UN-Women and OHCHR, *Violence against Women in Politics: Expert Group Meeting Report and Recommendations, 8–9 March 2018, New York* (2018); UNDP and UN-Women, *Preventing Violence against Women in Elections: A Programming Guide* (2017); and A/HRC/23/50.

that may prevent women from participating in elections. Means to discourage women's participation include psychological violence, such as threats or defamation, or physical or sexual violence. Women in political and public life are also regularly victims of technology-facilitated violence, especially on social media.

States have due diligence obligations to prevent, investigate and punish acts of violence against women in politics, whether they are perpetrated by State or non-State actors. In light of this, the Special Rapporteur on violence against women, its causes and consequences recommended that States adopt and implement legislation prohibiting and criminalizing violence against women in politics or incorporate adequate provisions into existing laws on eliminating violence against women, including online or ICT-facilitated violence, consistent with international and regional human rights standards. The Special Rapporteur recommended that States build the capacity of all State institutions, including parliaments and election bodies, to guarantee that women can work in security, free from gender-based violence, and strengthen complaint mechanisms and response protocols within such institutions and political parties in line with international and regional standards. Additionally, the Special Rapporteur recommended that States establish access to justice mechanisms and reparation measures for women victims of violence in politics, including compensation for victims or reinstatement for those who were forced to resign from public positions due to violence.[107]

Collecting and monitoring data on violence against women, including on femicide, in politics nationally and analysing this data is central to the design of prevention strategies. Efforts have been made to document, prevent and ultimately eliminate gender-based violence in electoral contexts, including through data collection and reporting of human rights violations, notably by the Special Rapporteur on violence against women, its causes and consequences[108] and UN-Women. Election observation and violence monitoring programmes, both at the international and the domestic levels, provide key opportunities for collecting information on violence against women in elections. Various international organizations have also developed tools to combat violence against women in politics.[109]

[107] For additional recommendations, see the Special Rapporteur's report on violence against women in politics (A/73/301), para. 83.

[108] Ibid.

[109] See UN-Women and OHCHR, *Violence against Women in Politics;* and UNDP and UN-Women, *Preventing Violence against Women in Elections.*

(g) *Right to a fair trial and an effective remedy*

65. The right to an effective remedy (Universal Declaration of Human Rights, art. 8; and International Covenant on Civil and Political Rights, art. 2 (3) (a)) and the right to a fair trial (Universal Declaration of Human Rights, art. 10; and International Covenant on Civil and Political Rights, art. 14) are fundamental to the protection of all other human rights, including the above-mentioned prerequisite rights. Therefore, they are essential both during and between election periods. Additionally, it is necessary to guarantee the rights to an effective remedy and to a fair trial to ensure effective avenues through which people can express objections and complaints regarding the electoral process. The relevant provisions of the International Covenant on Civil and Political Rights read as follows:

International Covenant on Civil and Political Rights

Article 2 (3) (a)

Each State Party to the present Covenant undertakes:

(a) To ensure that any person whose rights or freedoms as herein recognized are violated shall have an effective remedy, notwithstanding that the violation has been committed by persons acting in an official capacity;

Article 14 (1)

All persons shall be equal before the courts and tribunals. In the determination of any criminal charge against him, or of his rights and obligations in a suit at law, everyone shall be entitled to a fair and public hearing by a competent, independent and impartial tribunal established by law. ...

66. The right to an effective remedy requires States to ensure that individuals have access to independent and impartial tribunals, administrative mechanisms or other competent authorities. Moreover, the right to an effective remedy includes a right to reparation[110] for the harm suffered as a result of a violation of human rights. In its general comment No. 25 (1996), the Human Rights Committee

[110] Reparation can take the form of restitution, compensation, rehabilitation, satisfaction and guarantees of non-repetition. See Basic Principles and Guidelines on the Right to a Remedy and Reparation for Victims of Gross Violations of International Human Rights Law and Serious Violations of International Humanitarian Law.

held that there should be "access to judicial review or other equivalent process so that electors have confidence in the security of the ballot and the counting of the votes" (para. 20). Furthermore, the Committee has encouraged States parties to ensure universal access to complaint procedures and effective remedies in the event of contested election results.[111] As part of their duty to provide effective remedy and reparation, States parties have an obligation to take measures to prevent reoccurrence of violations, including ensuring that the regulatory framework for electoral processes is in line with article 25 of the International Covenant on Civil and Political Rights[112] and does not impose unreasonable restrictions on citizens' participation.[113]

67. The requirement of competence, independence and impartiality of a tribunal in the sense of article 14 (1) of the International Covenant on Civil and Political Rights is an absolute right that is not subject to any exceptions.[114] The notion of "tribunal" designates a body, regardless of its denomination, that is established by law, is independent of the executive and legislative or enjoys judicial independence in deciding legal matters.[115] Therefore, this may extend to electoral management bodies, which should observe these criteria when performing electoral dispute resolution functions.[116] An important aspect of a fair trial is its expeditiousness,[117] which is important in limited electoral time frames. In this regard, the Human Rights Committee has found that judicial proceedings that were politically motivated and instituted in order to prevent a candidate from running for presidential office violated the right to a fair trial and the right to political participation.[118] Finally, accountability mechanisms should be gender-sensitive to ensure the right of access to justice for women.[119]

---

[111] CCPR/C/MDG/CO/4, paras. 53–54.
[112] *Delgado Burgoa v. Plurinational State of Bolivia*, para. 13.
[113] *Staderini and De Lucia v. Italy*, para. 11.
[114] Human Rights Committee, general comment No. 32 (2007), para. 19.
[115] Ibid., para. 18.
[116] *Katashynskyi v. Ukraine* (CCPR/C/123/D/2250/2013), para. 7.2.
[117] Human Rights Committee, general comment No. 32 (2007), para. 27.
[118] *Nasheed v. Maldives*, paras. 8.3–8.6.
[119] Committee on the Elimination of Discrimination against Women, general recommendation No. 33 (2015).

(h) Right to education

68. Education is both a human right in itself and an indispensable means of realizing other human rights, including the right to political participation.[120] Education enables all persons to participate effectively in a free society.[121] To respect, protect and fulfil the right to education, States should ensure education in all its forms and at all levels exhibit the following interrelated and essential features: (a) availability of functioning educational institutions and programmes; (b) accessibility of education to everyone, without discrimination; (c) acceptability of form and substance; and (d) adaptability to the needs of changing societies and communities.[122]

69. Through education, States should empower rights holders to effectively exercise the right to participate in public affairs. United Nations guidance recommends that civic education programmes should be developed and implemented as an integral part of school curricula, in both public and private institutions.[123] Such programmes should aim to empower rights holders, promoting a culture of participation and building agency within local communities. Such programmes should also include knowledge of human rights, the importance of participation for society, and an understanding of the electoral and political system and of various opportunities for participation, including the available legislative, policy and institutional frameworks.[124] In line with the principles of accessibility and adaptability, it is important that civic education programmes be provided for individuals and groups that are marginalized or discriminated against and should take into account specific challenges, such as illiteracy and language and cultural barriers, in order to empower them to be active participants in public life.[125]

3. Specific social groups and special measures

70. States have an obligation to guarantee protection against discrimination and equal access to political participation for women and other social groups that face specific challenges, including (but not limited to) minorities and indigenous

---

[120] Committee on Economic, Social and Cultural Rights, general comment No. 13 (1999), para. 1.

[121] Ibid., para. 4. See also the United Nations Declaration on Human Rights Education and Training (General Assembly resolution 66/137).

[122] Committee on Economic, Social and Cultural Rights, general comment No. 13 (1999), para. 6.

[123] Guidelines for States on the effective implementation of the right to participate in public affairs, para. 24.

[124] Ibid.

[125] Ibid.

peoples, persons with disabilities, young persons, lesbian, gay, bisexual, transgender and intersex persons, people living in poverty and internally displaced persons.

71. In particular, States have an obligation to guarantee that women, as well as men, enjoy equal access to political participation with a view to ensuring equal representation in political and public life.[126] Participatory rights must be enjoyed by women both de jure and de facto.[127] This obligation requires States to adopt legal measures at all levels: constitutional, legislative and judicial.[128] Such measures include the adoption of temporary special measures, including quotas that are necessary to achieve equality between men and women in political and public life, in order to contend with the underlying structural disadvantaging of women.[129]

72. The Committee on the Elimination of Discrimination against Women has highlighted effective temporary strategies to achieve equality of participation, including a wide range of measures such as recruiting, financially assisting and training women candidates, amending electoral procedures and developing campaigns directed at equal participation.[130] Good practices of States include a legislative, and preferably constitutional, requirement that political parties place women in realistic positions for election, apply quotas and guarantee the rotation of power, accountability and parity membership between women and men on their governing boards and condition the funding of political parties on their integration of women in realistic positions on their candidate lists.[131] States should also address any indication of stagnation and segregation in the progress towards parity by designing and implementing innovative strategies to overcome specific barriers and enhancing the capacity to consistently and regularly monitor progress at all levels of decision-making across the whole spectrum of institutions of public and political life.[132] Also central is creating enabling conditions for public recognition and acceptance of

---

126 See, inter alia, CCPR/C/SLV/CO/7, para. 12; and CCPR/C/LBN/CO/3, para. 18. See also CEDAW/C/PAK/CO/4, paras. 25–26, on the forced disenfranchisement of women and factors that impede and discourage women's participation in elections as voters and as candidates. See also A/57/38(SUPP), paras. 402–403, on the low rate of registration of women as voters and their low representation on electoral lists in Yemen.

127 Committee on the Elimination of Discrimination against Women, general recommendation No. 23 (1997), para. 18.

128 A/HRC/23/50, paras. 77 and 97.

129 Convention on the Elimination of All Forms of Discrimination against Women, arts. 4, 7 and 8. See also Committee on the Elimination of Discrimination against Women, general recommendation No. 25 (2004) and general recommendation No. 23 (1997), para. 18; and A/HRC/23/50, para. 38.

130 Committee on the Elimination of Discrimination against Women, general recommendation No. 23 (1997).

131 A/HRC/23/50, para. 76.

132 Ibid., para. 97.

women in positions of leadership and decision-making through public campaigns and educational programmes that are responsive to multicultural settings. This includes providing a positive image of diverse women, including minority women, indigenous women, women with disabilities and other historically marginalized women, in leadership and decision-making positions.[133]

73. As regards lesbian, gay, bisexual, transgender and intersex persons, it should be noted that everyone, irrespective of sexual orientation, gender identity or sex characteristics, is entitled to enjoy the protection of international human rights law, including as regards the right to political participation. Lesbian, gay, bisexual, transgender and intersex persons sometimes face specific barriers and may suffer human rights violations in the context of elections based on their sexual orientation, gender identity or sex characteristics. Violations may include homophobic, transphobic or biphobic attacks and violence, discrimination in law or in practice or non-recognition of the self-determined gender of transgender persons.[134] United Nations human rights mechanisms have confirmed that sexual orientation, gender identity and sex characteristics are included among the prohibited grounds of discrimination under international human rights law.[135]

74. With regard to minorities, States also have an obligation to guarantee their full enjoyment of participation rights, including protection against discrimination.[136] To that end, States should adopt an electoral framework that guarantees equal enjoyment of the right to political participation irrespective of minority status, and remove provisions that discriminate against citizens from certain minority groups by preventing them from fully participating in elections.[137]

---

133 Ibid.

134 See A/HRC/29/23.

135 Committee on Economic, Social and Cultural Rights, general comment No. 20 (2009), para. 32; CCPR/C/TUN/CO/6, para. 16; CCPR/C/SEN/CO/5, para. 11; CCPR/C/VNM/CO/3, para. 14; and Human Rights Committee, *Toonen v. Australia*, communication No. 488/1992. See also A/HRC/35/36, para. 20.

136 CCPR/C/THA/CO/2, para. 44; and CCPR/C/FRA/CO/5, paras. 13–14.

137 International Covenant on Civil and Political Rights, art. 25; and Declaration on the Rights of Persons Belonging to National or Ethnic, Religious and Linguistic Minorities, art. 2 (2) and (3). The link between the rights of people belonging to minorities and the right to participate in public affairs is further strengthened by article 27 of the International Covenant on Civil and Political Rights, which explicitly recognizes minority rights. See also CCPR/C/BIH/CO/3, para. 12; CCPR/C/ALB/CO/2, para. 23, on ensuring that all Roma have identity cards so as to facilitate their right to vote; CCPR/C/HUN/CO/5, para. 21 ("the State party should adopt measures to address the shortcomings of the minority election register"); and CERD/C/IND/CO/19, para. 17 ("many Dalits are not included in electoral rolls or otherwise denied the right to vote").

Political participation of minorities and indigenous peoples

International human rights norms and standards protect the right of minorities to participate in the conduct of public affairs.[138] Specific provisions address the participation rights of minorities that are also indigenous peoples, including the right to self-determination and the right to free, prior and informed consent on issues that affect them.[139] On this basis, the Human Rights Committee has stated that the participation of a minority or indigenous community in the decision-making process must be effective, which requires not mere consultation but the free, prior and informed consent of the members of the community.[140] Furthermore, the Committee has also stated that the enjoyment of minority rights may require positive legal measures of protection and measures to ensure the effective participation of members of minority communities in decisions that affect them.[141] Therefore, any mechanism for participation should be genuine and inclusive and consultation processes should include wide participation from within the minority community.

However, persons belonging to minority and indigenous groups are frequently excluded from political participation and underrepresented in political life.[142] To remedy this situation, different institutional arrangements have been designed in various countries to ensure the effective participation of persons belonging to minority groups in political life. The extent to which the design of an electoral system might have an impact on minority participation and representation depends considerably on the country-specific context. Nevertheless, various measures may be considered, such as a system of proportional representation to ensure the representation of diverse political parties in proportion to their popularity, the introduction of lower threshold requirements for minority political parties, reserved seats for minorities, an assessment of the effects of political parties' candidate selection processes on the participation of minorities and the delimitation of the boundaries of electoral districts.

---

138 Declaration on the Rights of Persons Belonging to National or Ethnic, Religious and Linguistic Minorities, art. 2. See annex I below.

139 United Nations Declaration on the Rights of Indigenous Peoples, arts. 3 and 41. See also CCPR/C/NOR/CO/7, para. 37 (b); and E/C.12/AUS/CO/5, para. 16 (e).

140 *Poma Poma v. Peru* (CCPR/C/95/D/1457/2006), para. 7.6. See also A/HRC/39/62.

141 Human Rights Committee, general comment No. 23 (1994), para. 7.

142 UNDP, *Marginalised Minorities in Development Programming* (New York, 2010), p. 24.

> The United Nations Declaration on the Rights of Indigenous Peoples underlined that indigenous peoples also have the right to maintain and strengthen their distinct political, legal, economic, social and cultural institutions, while retaining their right to participate fully, if they so choose, in the political, economic, social and cultural life of the State.[143]

75. Similarly, the Human Rights Committee has held that States have an obligation to ensure that persons with disabilities are not discriminated against on the basis of their actual or perceived impairments, regardless of intellectual, mental, physical or sensory impairment, and that they are provided with the support necessary to exercise in practice all of the rights set out in article 25 of the International Covenant on Civil and Political Rights.[144] Article 29 of the Convention on the Rights of Persons with Disabilities requires States parties to ensure that persons with disabilities can effectively and fully participate in political and public life on an equal basis with others, including by guaranteeing their right to vote and stand for election. Article 29 does not foresee any reasonable restrictions, nor does it allow any exception for any group of persons with disabilities. Therefore, an exclusion of the right to vote on the basis of a perceived or actual psychosocial or intellectual disability, including a restriction pursuant to an individualized assessment, constitutes discrimination on the basis of disability.[145] The guidelines for States on the effective implementation of the right to participate in public affairs provide that States should ensure that all persons with disabilities, especially those with intellectual or psychosocial disabilities, may exercise their right to vote.[146] The Convention on the Rights of Persons with Disabilities recommends that accessibility and reasonable accommodation for persons with disabilities be provided at all stages of the electoral cycle to facilitate the exercise of the right to vote in private or through a chosen assistant.[147] To this end, States

---

[143] United Nations Declaration on the Rights of Indigenous Peoples, art. 5.

[144] Human Rights Committee, *Ignatane v. Latvia*, communication No. 884/1999, para. 7.4. See also, inter alia, CCPR/C/BGR/CO/4, para. 18; CCPR/C/LTU/CO/4, para. 14; CCPR/C/GTM/CO/4, para. 27; and CCPR/C/AUS/CO/6, para. 48.

[145] *Bujdosó et al. v. Hungary* (CRPD/C/10/D/4/2011), para. 9.4. See also Committee on the Rights of Persons with Disabilities, general comment No. 1 (2014), para. 48. The Special Rapporteur on the rights of persons with disabilities also considers that "no one should be restricted, either in law or in practice, in the enjoyment of political rights on the grounds of disability" (A/HRC/31/62, para. 19).

[146] Para. 38.

[147] CRPD/C/GBR/CO/1, para. 61.

have an ex ante duty to ensure accessibility, meaning they should ensure accessibility before receiving an individual request to enter or use a place or service.[148] Inaccessible voting processes hinder the participation of persons with disabilities in elections. The denial or restriction of legal capacity often triggers a denial of political rights, especially the right to vote, for certain persons with disabilities.[149] The report of the Special Rapporteur on the rights of persons with disabilities stressed that States must eliminate, in law and in practice, all denials or restrictions of legal capacity of persons with disabilities in the exercise of these rights.[150]

76. For its part, the Forum on Human Rights, Democracy and the Rule of Law, mandated by the Human Rights Council,[151] recommends that the political participation of young persons,[152] a group that is largely underrepresented in political life, should be ensured without discrimination, with particular attention given to young persons with disabilities, young women and girls and young human rights defenders.[153] As regards people living in poverty, the Committee on Economic, Social and Cultural Rights considers that the mere holding of elections is not enough to ensure that they enjoy their right to participate in key decisions affecting their lives and stresses that participatory processes should be informed by reliable, disaggregated data and designed and implemented by appropriately trained officials.[154]

77. International standards allow temporary special measures in order to correct past discrimination and promote political participation by groups that face structural inequalities. Those groups include women, minorities, persons with

---

[148] Committee on the Rights of Persons with Disabilities, general comment No. 2 (2014). See also *Given v. Australia* (CRPD/C/19/D/19/2014), para. 8.5.

[149] Committee on the Rights of Persons with Disabilities, general comment No. 1 (2014), para. 48.

[150] A/HRC/37/56, para. 25.

[151] In its resolution 28/14, adopted on 26 March 2015, the Human Rights Council decided to establish a forum on human rights, democracy and rule of law. The purpose of the Forum is "to provide a platform for promoting dialogue and cooperation on issues pertaining to the relationship between these areas" and to "identify and analyse best practices, challenges and opportunities for States in their efforts to secure respect for human rights, democracy and the rule of law" (ibid., para. 1).

[152] Most United Nations entities, including the General Assembly, define youth (or young persons) as the population segment between 15 and 24 years of age.

[153] A/HRC/34/46, paras. 21–30. See also UNDP, *Enhancing Youth Political Participation Throughout the Electoral Cycle: A Good Practice Guide* (2013).

[154] E/C.12/2001/10, para. 12.

disabilities and persons living in rural or remote areas.[155] The Human Rights Committee has clarified that "not all differentiation constitutes discrimination if it is based on objective and reasonable criteria and the purpose sought is legitimate under the Covenant".[156] Similarly, article 4 (1) of the Convention on the Elimination of All Forms of Discrimination against Women provides for the adoption of "temporary special measures" aimed at accelerating de facto equality between men and women.[157] Furthermore, article 5 of the Convention on the Rights of Persons with Disabilities enables "specific measures" for persons with disabilities that may be temporary or permanent and that aim at correcting structural discrimination.[158] Temporary special measures include a wide variety of legislative, executive, administrative and other regulatory instruments, policies and practices, such as preferential treatment and quotas.[159]

Political participation of internally displaced persons

Internally displaced persons often face barriers to exercise their right to take part in the conduct of public affairs, to vote and to be elected. As the political participation of citizens and residents is often regulated according to their location, individuals face obstacles to political participation in the context of internal displacement. Issues related to identification, including lack of documentation, destroyed, lost or confiscated documents, restrictions on movement, insecurity, restrictive residency requirements for registration for elections, the lack of an inclusive legal framework and the lack of timely information and appropriate arrangements pose obstacles for internally displaced persons to participate in elections. On the other hand, electoral disputes and exclusion from political participation may also be the cause of internal displacement or hinder the return, local integration or settlement of internally displaced persons elsewhere in the country.[160]

---

155 International Convention on the Elimination of All Forms of Racial Discrimination, art. 1 (4); Convention on the Elimination of All Forms of Discrimination against Women, art. 4 (1); Convention on the Rights of Persons with Disabilities, art. 5 (4); and CERD/C/64/CO/5, para. 17. See also guidelines for States on the effective implementation of the right to participate in public affairs, para. 31.

156 *Gillot et al. v. France* (CCPR/C/75/D/932/2000), para. 13.5.

157 See also Committee on the Elimination of Discrimination against Women, general recommendation No. 25 (2004) and general recommendation No. 23 (1997), para. 15.

158 Committee on the Rights of Persons with Disabilities, general comment No. 6 (2018), para. 28.

159 Committee on the Elimination of Discrimination against Women, general recommendation No. 25 (2004), para. 22.

160 See, for example, the report of the Global Protection Cluster and the Carter Center, "Public and political participation of internally displaced persons", in which the presentations and discussions during a round table held in Amman in October 2018 are summarized. Available at www.globalprotectioncluster.org/wp-content/uploads/Public-and-Political-Participation-of-IDPs.pdf.

As recalled by the Special Rapporteur on the human rights of internally displaced persons, internally displaced persons do not lose their right to participate because they have had to leave their homes, and measures must be taken to protect those rights during displacement.[161] The Guiding Principles on Internal Displacement state that internally displaced persons shall enjoy, in full equality, the same rights and freedoms under domestic and internal law as do other persons in their country and shall not be discriminated against in the enjoyment of any rights and freedoms on the grounds that they are internally displaced persons (principle 1). Principle 22 states that internally displaced persons, whether or not they live in camps, shall not be discriminated against as a result of their displacement in the enjoyment of their right to vote and to participate in governmental and public affairs, including the right to have access to the means necessary to exercise this right. Also relevant to electoral participation, principle 20 addresses the issuance of documentation for internally displaced persons necessary for the enjoyment and exercise of their legal rights, in particular the issuance of new documents or the replacement of documents lost during displacement.

4. States of emergency

78. Holding elections during or in the aftermath of a public emergency brings challenges as some fundamental rights may be curtailed. The International Covenant on Civil and Political Rights provides for strict criteria under which human rights can be restricted or derogated from. Article 4 reads as follows:

International Covenant on Civil and Political Rights

Article 4

1. In time of public emergency which threatens the life of the nation and the existence of which is officially proclaimed, the States Parties to the present Covenant may take measures derogating from their obligations under the present Covenant to the extent strictly required by the exigencies of the situation, provided that such measures are not inconsistent with their other obligations under international law and do not involve discrimination solely on the ground of race, colour, sex, language, religion or social origin.

[161] A/72/202, para. 17.

2. No derogation from articles 6, 7, 8 (paragraphs 1 and 2), 11, 15, 16 and 18 may be made under this provision.

3. Any State Party to the present Covenant availing itself of the right of derogation shall immediately inform the other States Parties to the present Covenant, through the intermediary of the Secretary-General of the United Nations, of the provisions from which it has derogated and of the reasons by which it was actuated. A further communication shall be made, through the same intermediary, on the date on which it terminates such derogation.

79. Periods of democratic transition often follow national emergencies, both declared and de facto. Emergency or other exceptional legislation restricting or derogating from fundamental rights will be generally inconsistent with the conduct of free elections. States preparing for elections should carefully review the impact of such legislation on the electoral process and consider the repeal or suspension of emergency measures.

80. International human rights law recognizes extraordinary measures may be required in times of public emergency. Limitations on certain rights, such as freedom of movement, freedom of expression or freedom of peaceful assembly, may be permissible so long as they meet the requirements of legality, necessity and proportionality, and non-discrimination. When proportionate limitations are not sufficient, derogation from or suspension of certain rights is permitted following the declaration of a state of emergency.

81. A state of emergency should be declared only in accordance with the law and authorized only in the event of a public emergency that threatens the life of the nation, where measures compatible with the Constitution and laws in force are plainly inadequate to address the situation. In every case, States should adopt legislation that carefully and clearly defines the extent to which the constitutional order may be altered in the event of an emergency situation.

82. Furthermore, relevant international norms and standards require that a state of emergency be officially proclaimed before any derogation measures are put into place.[162] Any such measures must be strictly required by the exigencies of the situation. This requirement relates to the duration, geographical coverage and

[162] Human Rights Committee, general comment No. 29 (2001), para. 2. See also Siracusa Principles on the Limitation and Derogation Provisions in the International Covenant on Civil and Political Rights, paras. 42–44.

substantive basis of the state of emergency. Measures must not discriminate solely on the basis of race, colour, sex, language, religion or social origin and must not be inconsistent with other requirements under international law.

83. A number of rights may not be subject to any derogation or suspension, even in times of emergency.[163] These include the right to life, the prohibition of torture and ill-treatment, the prohibition of imprisonment because of an inability to fulfil a contractual obligation, the principle of legality in the field of criminal law, the recognition of everyone as a person before the law, freedom of thought, conscience and religion and the prohibition of the death penalty for States that are parties to the Second Optional Protocol to the International Covenant on Civil and Political Rights, aiming at the abolition of the death penalty. The Human Rights Committee has commented that the prohibition of any kind of political dissent is not compatible with the provisions of the International Covenant on Civil and Political Rights on states of emergency.[164]

B. Genuine elections

84. The *travaux préparatoires* of the International Covenant on Civil and Political Rights indicate that the framers of the instrument saw "genuine elections" as comprising two broad elements. The first is procedural, and includes the guarantees of periodicity, equality and universality of suffrage, and secrecy of the ballot.[165] The second element is outcome-oriented, and defines genuine elections as those that reflect and give effect to the free expression of the will of the people[166] and in which voters have a certain minimum amount of political influence.[167] In the words of the Human Rights Committee, "the results of genuine elections should be respected and implemented."[168]

---

163 International Covenant on Civil and Political Rights, art. 4 (2). See also Human Rights Committee, general comment No. 29 (2001), para. 7.

164 Human Rights Committee, *Silva et al. v. Uruguay*, communication No. 34/1978, para. 8.4.

165 See, for example, A/C.3/SR.1096 and A/C.3/SR.1097.

166 See A/C.3/SR.1096.

167 William A. Schabas, *Nowak's CCPR Commentary: U.N. International Covenant on Civil and Political Rights*, 3rd ed. (Kehl, Engel Verlag, 2019), p. 710.

168 Human Rights Committee, general comment No. 25 (1996), para. 19.

1. Periodicity and the electoral time frame

(a) Periodicity

85. The requirement that elections be held periodically is expressly stated in the Universal Declaration of Human Rights (art. 21 (3)) and the International Covenant on Civil and Political Rights (art. 25 (b)). While no particular schedule of periodicity is set by the instruments, the Human Rights Committee has indicated that "elections must be held at intervals which are not unduly long and which ensure that the authority of government continues to be based on the free expression of the will of electors",[169] which is the basis of governmental legitimacy.

86. The importance of this provision should not be minimized. Once-only elections (e.g. when a country gains independence or when it transitions from an authoritarian regime) will not suffice for international human rights purposes. Rather, this provision makes clear that a sustained democratic order is required, which is continually answerable to the will of the people.

(b) Postponing elections

87. Postponement of scheduled elections may occur for various reasons. When necessitated by a public emergency, it may be permitted in certain limited circumstances, but only if and to the extent strictly required by the exigencies of the situation (see paras. 78–83 above on states of emergency). Any such extraordinary measures must comply with all the international standards for such derogations and must not threaten democracy itself.[170] Any decision to postpone elections must be based on broad consultations and conditions must be in place to foster and ensure an inclusive dialogue and reach political consensus. Participation of oppositions groups, as well as of women and other traditionally marginalized groups, in the dialogue must be ensured.

(c) The electoral calendar

88. An adequate and realistic electoral calendar is important so that each phase of the process allows for the effective exercise of the right to vote and be elected, as well as all other prerequisite rights by ensuring adequate time

[169] Ibid., para. 9.

[170] International Covenant on Civil and Political Rights, art. 4.

for effective campaigning and public information efforts, voter registration, voter education and for the necessary administrative, legal, training and logistic arrangements to be made. It is important that the electoral calendar be publicized as part of civic information activities, in the interests of transparency and of securing public understanding and confidence in the process. An adequate and realistic electoral calendar is needed in view of the obligation of States to give effect to the rights recognized in international human rights treaties.[171]

2. Universal and equal suffrage

89. Relevant international standards focus on who must be permitted to participate in elections. Accordingly, the Universal Declaration of Human Rights (arts. 2 and 21 (3)) and the International Covenant on Civil and Political Rights (arts. 2 and 25 (b)) provide that suffrage must be non-discriminatory, equal and universal.

(a) Universal suffrage

90. Universal suffrage requires that the broadest reasonable pool of voters be guaranteed participatory rights. The Human Rights Committee has indicated that the exercise of the right to vote should be available to every adult citizen.[172] The Committee has also indicated that any conditions that apply to the exercise of the rights protected by article 25 of the International Covenant on Civil and Political Rights should be based on objective and reasonable criteria. For example, the Committee has indicated that it may be reasonable to require a higher age for election or appointment to particular offices than for exercising the right to vote[173] or to set a minimum age for the right to vote.[174] Unreasonable restrictions on universal suffrage include, but are not limited to, those based on:

---

[171] Ibid., art. 2 (2); Convention on the Elimination of All Forms of Discrimination against Women, art. 2 (e) and (f); Convention on the Rights of Persons with Disabilities, art. 4 (a)–(c); and Human Rights Committee, general comment No. 25 (1996), para. 1.

[172] Human Rights Committee, general comment No. 25 (1996), para. 4.

[173] Ibid.

[174] Ibid., para. 10

(a) Economic requirements, based notably on property ownership;[175]

(b) Excessive residency requirements;[176]

(c) Restrictions on voting by naturalized citizens (as opposed to citizens by birth);[177]

(d) Language requirements;[178]

(e) Educational requirements;[179]

(f) Literacy requirements;[180]

(g) Party membership;[181]

(h) Excessive limitations on the voting rights of convicted criminals;[182]

(i) Disability.[183]

(b) Equal suffrage

91. Equal suffrage is the idea usually expressed as "one person, one vote". When conducting constituency delimitation, efforts should be made so that the votes of individuals, groups or geographic areas are equally weighted in light of the international norm of equality of suffrage.[184] Voter registration and polling procedures should ensure that the processes only allow each person to have one vote. Group voting, including family voting and proxy voting, may particularly hamper women's equal participation in elections. In short, each vote must carry equal weight.

---

[175] Ibid.

[176] Ibid., para. 11. See also CCPR/C/UZB/CO/4, para. 26 (long-residency requirement).

[177] Human Rights Committee, general comment No. 25 (1996), para. 3. See also CCPR/C/KWT/CO/3, paras. 46–47.

[178] International Covenant on Civil and Political Rights, art. 2. See also CCPR/C/UZB/CO/4, para. 26.

[179] Human Rights Committee, general comment No. 25 (1996), para. 10.

[180] Ibid.

[181] Ibid.

[182] Ibid., para. 14. See also *Yevdokimov and Rezanov v. Russian Federation*, para. 7.5; CCPR/C/EST/CO/4, para. 34; CCPR/C/TKM/CO/2, para. 51; CCPR/C/GBR/CO/7, para. 25; and CCPR/C/KHM/CO/2, para. 26. See also guidelines for States on the effective implementation of the right to participate in public affairs, para. 42.

[183] Convention on the Rights of Persons with Disabilities, art. 29. See also Human Rights Committee, general comment No. 25 (1996), para. 10; CCPR/C/LTU/CO/4, para. 14; CCPR/C/GTM/CO/4, para. 27; and CCPR/C/AUS/CO/6, para. 48. See also *Bujdosó et al. v. Hungary*, para. 9.4; and CRPD/C/PER/CO/1, para. 45. See also guidelines for States on the effective implementation of the right to participate in public affairs, para. 38.

[184] Human Rights Committee, general comment No. 25 (1996), para. 21. See also CCPR/C/CHN-MAC/CO/1, para. 7; CCPR/C/CHL/CO/5, para. 15; CEDAW/C/TJK/CO/3, para. 26 (family voting); and *Mátyus v. Slovakia* (CCPR/C/75/D/923/2000), paras. 9.2 and 10.

3. Secret ballot

92. The requirement that elections be held by secret ballot originates in the Universal Declaration of Human Rights (art. 21 (3)). The obligation to guarantee the secrecy of the ballot also features in the International Covenant on Civil and Political Rights (art. 25 (b)). States should take measures to guarantee the requirement of the secrecy of the vote during elections, including absentee voting, in situations in which such a system exists.[185] This requirement implies that voters should be protected from any form of coercion or compulsion to disclose how they intend to vote or how they voted, and from any unlawful or arbitrary interference with the voting process.[186] Furthermore, the vote should remain secret at all stages of the process, including during voting, counting and the tabulation of results. To ensure that persons with disabilities can exercise the right to vote on an equal basis with others, the Convention on the Rights of Persons with Disabilities (art. 29 (a) (ii)) allows for the provision of assistance in voting to persons with disabilities, strictly by a person of their own choice.

4. Genuine effect

93. Genuine elections are those that reveal and give effect to the freely expressed will of the people and succeed in providing genuine inclusion and effective representation for all of the diverse aspects of the public.[187] For the outcome to be accepted, people must have confidence that it reflects their will. Elections must be designed to bring about the transfer of power to prevailing candidates in accordance with a prearranged formula acceptable to the people.

94. The transfer of power to those elected must be both committed to by the ruling and opposing parties and the subject of legal provisions for its implementation. In other words, elections must be subject only to the rule of law, and not to the whim of the existing Government or of any single party. Moreover, the elected authorities must be able to exercise the power conferred on them by law.

---

185 Human Rights Committee, general comment No. 25 (1996), para. 20.

186 Ibid. See also *Given v. Australia*.

187 Human Rights Committee, general comment No. 25 (1996), para. 21.

5. Real choice

95. Genuine elections also offer an actual choice to the electorate. While this does not presuppose any particular political system, real popular input must be institutionally accommodated. Both the Universal Declaration of Human Rights and the International Covenant on Civil and Political Rights prohibit discrimination on the basis of "political or other opinion" in the enjoyment of the right to take part in government, the right of freedom of association and the right of assembly. Political pluralism is an essential element in providing a real choice to the electors, and the Human Rights Committee gives importance to this in its consideration of reports submitted by States parties to the Covenant. For example, the Committee has held that States parties have an obligation to foster a culture of political pluralism and ensure a genuinely pluralistic political debate and should not attempt to exclude opposition candidates from electoral processes.[188] The Special Rapporteur on the promotion and protection of the right to freedom of opinion and expression has also highlighted that States should promote plurality and encourage a diverse and pluralistic political process that is hospitable to ideologies from across the political spectrum.[189]

96. Political pluralism also requires that parties be able to function effectively. To that end, legal protection for their full participation should be in place and electoral legislation should provide for fair and transparent funding of political campaigns (which may include some form of public financing).

---

188 See, inter alia, CCPR/C/GNQ/CO/1, para. 59; CCPR/C/SWZ/CO/1, para. 53; and CCPR/C/UZB/CO/4, para. 26.

189 A/HRC/26/30, para. 48.

6. Informed choice

97. An informed choice, whereby everyone has the right to seek and receive information, is essential for the concept of a "free" choice. If elections are to be genuine, they should reflect the political will of the people. Through access to information about the candidates and their proposed programmes, the parties and the electoral process, voters are in a position to freely formulate and express their will. The Human Rights Committee has stated that "the free communication of information and ideas about public and political issues between citizens, candidates and elected representatives is essential. This implies a free press and other media able to comment on public issues without censorship or restraint and to inform public opinion."[190]

98. Well-organized, non-partisan voter information programmes and unhindered distribution of political platforms and messages are therefore critical elements of genuine elections. Non-partisan education should aim to inform voters as to the "who, what, when, where and how" of the electoral process and polling. It should also help to inform the public on issues such as why they should participate and what measures are in place to protect their right to participate confidently in the process.[191]

99. Voter information should be accessible to all members of society, regardless of their language, level of literacy or impairments. To increase accessibility, when possible, it is important that voter education materials be multimedia, multilingual and culturally appropriate for various social groups. Furthermore, information and materials about voting should be available in minority languages.[192] Moreover, the electoral process and the voting facilities and materials should be adequate, accessible and easy to understand and use by persons with disabilities.[193] Where possible, this may include the provision of ballots and materials in accessible formats, such as Braille, sign language and easy-to-read formats.[194]

---

[190] Human Rights Committee, general comment No. 25 (1996), para. 25.
[191] Electoral management bodies often have a key role in voter information work.
[192] Human Rights Committee, general comment No. 25 (1996), para. 12.
[193] Convention on the Rights of Persons with Disabilities, art. 29 (a) (i). See also *Given v. Australia*.
[194] CRPD/C/IRQ/CO/1, para. 54 (b); CRPD/C/TUR/CO/1, para. 57 (b); and CRPD/C/LUX/CO/1, para. 51 (b).

100. The digital space has brought radical changes to communications, in particular in the political sphere. The proliferation of digital tools for censoring information and spreading disinformation represents a challenge to the quality of information necessary to make an informed choice.195 This may impact the ability of voters to form opinions independently, free of violence or the threat of violence, compulsion, inducement or manipulative interference of any kind.196

101. Access to the mass media should also be guaranteed to political parties and candidates, and such access should be fairly distributed. In addition, the use of media for campaign purposes should be responsible in terms of content, such that no party makes statements that constitute an incitement to violence. Further information on media access and regulation is provided in chapter IV below.

Impact of big data manipulation and social media on elections

New challenges to elections have arisen in the digital age,[197] notably information disorder[198] and big data manipulation. While the human right to impart information and ideas is not limited to "correct" statements, and protects information and ideas that may shock, offend and disturb,[199] widespread disinformation may pose significant threats to the right to political participation, both in relation to the right to participate in public affairs and to stand for elections and vote. Social media platforms have become key for

[195] Special Rapporteur on the promotion and protection of the right to freedom of opinion and expression of the United Nations, the Representative on Freedom of the Media of the Organization for Security and Cooperation in Europe, the Special Rapporteur for Freedom of Expression of the Organization of American States and the Special Rapporteur on Freedom of Expression and Access to Information of the African Commission on Human and Peoples' Rights, Joint declaration on freedom of expression and "fake news", disinformation and propaganda, 3 March 2017.

[196] Human Rights Committee, general comment No. 25 (1996), para. 19.

[197] Special Rapporteur on the promotion and protection of the right to freedom of opinion and expression, "Freedom of expression and elections in the digital age". See also Tarlach McGonagle and others, *Elections and Media in Digital Times* (Paris, UNESCO, 2019).

[198] See Claire Wardle and Hossein Derakhshan, *Information Disorder: Toward an Interdisciplinary Framework for Research and Policy Making* (Strasbourg, Council of Europe, 2017). In the report, the authors identify three different types of information disorder: misinformation (when false information is shared, but no harm is meant); disinformation (when false information is knowingly shared to cause harm); and mal-information (when genuine information is shared to cause harm, often by moving information designed to stay private into the public sphere).

[199] Joint declaration on freedom of expression and "fake news", disinformation and propaganda, seventh preambular paragraph and para. 2 (a).

political actors to disseminate disinformation, often helped by the preference of content curation algorithms for sensationalist content and the possibility to micro-target political advertising. In the context of electoral processes, social media may be instrumentalized to influence the outcomes of elections by discrediting candidates and political parties, providing incorrect information about the voting process (vote suppression) and seeking to influence the voting choices of particular segments of society that may be targeted based on patterns suggested by the processing of personal data and social media activity.

Disinformation may result in prerequisite rights to free and genuine elections being violated. For example, hate speech and discrimination can be amplified by online disinformation campaigns and may in turn lead to risks to the security of person and hate crimes. Freedom of expression and access to information may also be affected if a voter only has access to news through one social media platform that predominantly or only contains disinformation. Disseminating disinformation may lead to reducing understanding among people with different opinions or backgrounds and exacerbating polarization, playing on and distorting people's negative views of others. It can be used to splinter and manipulate public discourse, depriving voters of critical information for their decision-making.

While disinformation constitutes a real challenge in the electoral context, States should refrain from general and ambiguous prohibition of the dissemination of information, such as "falsehoods" or "non-objective information". Such terms do not adequately describe the content that is prohibited. As a result, they provide the authorities with a broad remit to censor the expression of unpopular, controversial or minority opinions, as well as criticism of the Government and politicians in the media and during electoral campaigns. Human rights experts have recommended that approaches to combat disinformation should avoid criminalization and be instead evidence-based and tailored to the proven or documented impacts of disinformation and propaganda. These measures could include the promotion of independent fact-checking mechanisms, the provision of support for independent and diverse public service media outlets, public education and digital literacy campaigns.[200]

[200] Special Rapporteur on the promotion and protection of the right to freedom of opinion and expression, "Freedom of expression and elections in the digital age", p. 11.

C. Other requirements/safeguarding public freedoms and the integrity of electoral processes

1. Role of police and security forces

102. Police and other security forces play a dual role in an election setting. Effective law enforcement during an election period requires a balance between the need for electoral security and maintenance of order and non-interference with fundamental freedoms and participation rights to maintain or create an environment free of intimidation. In the light of past examples of electoral-related sexual violence, particular measures need to be taken to ensure a safe environment for women voters and candidates.[201] The Code of Conduct for Law Enforcement Officials imposes a duty of service to the community upon all officers of the law (art. 1) and provides that "law enforcement officials shall respect and protect human dignity and maintain and uphold the human rights of all persons" (art. 2).[202] This necessarily requires that security forces strive to ensure that all citizens benefit from elections that are administratively sound and free of any disruptive forces that seek to undermine the free expression of popular will.

103. In addition, the Code of Conduct requires law enforcement officials to "rigorously oppose and combat" any act of corruption (art. 7). This may suggest a duty to prevent attempts at election fraud, personation, bribery, intimidation or any other acts that law enforcement officials may witness. The Code of Conduct also provides that law enforcement officials "shall not commit any act of corruption" (art. 7).

104. In every case, any police presence outside places of registration or polling should be discreet, professional and impartial. Political leadership should refrain from attempting to unduly influence law enforcement operations, actions and decisions.[203] The Human Rights Committee has also indicated that States have an obligation to ensure that law enforcement personnel do not use unnecessary

---

[201] See OHCHR, UN-Women and Physicians for Human Rights, "Breaking cycles of violence: gaps in prevention of and response to electoral related sexual violence".

[202] Code of Conduct for Law Enforcement Officials adopted by the General Assembly in its resolution 34/169 of 17 December 1979. See also the Basic Principles on the Use of Force and Firearms by Law Enforcement Officials adopted by the Eighth United Nations Congress on the Prevention of Crime and the Treatment of Offenders in 1990, paras. 12–13.

[203] OHCHR and United Nations Office on Drugs and Crime, *Resource Book on the Use of Force and Firearms in Law Enforcement* (New York, 2017), p. 25.

or disproportionate force and to abide by international norms and standards on the use of force, including by providing such personnel with training, taking due account of the Basic Principles on the Use of Force and Firearms by Law Enforcement Officials.[204]

2. Role of election observers

105. The General Assembly has acknowledged the importance of national and international observation of elections for the promotion of free and fair elections and its contribution to enhancing the integrity of electoral processes in requesting countries, promoting public confidence and electoral participation and mitigating the potential for election-related disturbances.[205] Election observers can provide an effective means of assessing the electoral process against existing standards and obligations, national law and good practice. Furthermore, election observers from national NGOs and international organizations can help promote public confidence in the electoral process. As stated by the Human Rights Committee, "there should be independent scrutiny of the voting and counting process ... so that electors have confidence in the security of the ballot and the counting of the votes."[206] The presence of observers may prevent or decrease the likelihood of fraud, intimidation and violence.

106. Election observation is in itself part of the right to participate in public affairs.[207] Whether drawn from international or regional intergovernmental organizations, NGOs, political parties or official missions from other States, observers should be afforded freedom of movement and access to polling stations throughout the country[208] and protected from harm and interference in their official duties.[209] Observers should integrate a gender perspective into electoral observation and monitoring and be aware of the challenges faced by other traditionally marginalized groups or other groups at risk in this context and ensure that they are informed about the local context and culture.

---

[204] CCPR/C/AGO/CO/2, para. 26; CCPR/C/SDN/CO/5, para. 48; and CCPR/C/COD/CO/4, para. 44. See also *Guidance on Less-Lethal Weapons in Law Enforcement* (United Nations publication, 2020).

[205] General Assembly resolution 74/158, preamble.

[206] Human Rights Committee, general comment No. 25 (1996), para. 20. See also CCPR/C/HND/CO/2, para. 45.

[207] Declaration of Principles for International Election Observation (2005), para. 16.

[208] Guidelines for States on the effective implementation of the right to participate in public affairs, para. 44. See also CCPR/C/IRN/CO/3, para. 29 ("international observers were not allowed entry to monitor the election results"); and Declaration of Principles for International Electoral Observation, para. 12 (d)–(e).

[209] Declaration of Principles for International Electoral Observation, para. 12 (h)–(i).

3. Prevention of corruption

107. As pointed out by the Human Rights Committee, States parties to the International Covenant on Civil and Political Rights have an obligation under article 25 to fight and eradicate corruption to guarantee effective participation in public affairs.[210] States should ensure that all cases of corruption are independently and impartially investigated so that corruption does not go unpunished.[211] Prevention of corruption also entails transparency in campaign financing.[212] Transparency in the disclosure of campaign financing and expenditure and access to information need to ensure equality among all candidates, including members of the opposition, and parties so that voters are presented with a free choice.[213]

[210] CCPR/C/CMR/CO/5, para. 10; CCPR/C/DOM/CO/6, para. 30; and CCPR/C/BIH/CO/3, para. 12.

[211] CCPR/C/NER/CO/2, para. 11; and CCPR/C/AGO/CO/2, para. 12.

[212] United Nations Convention against Corruption, art. 7 (3). Chapter II of the Convention is dedicated to prevention, with measures directed at both the public and private sectors. These include model preventive policies, such as the establishment of anti-corruption bodies and enhanced transparency in the financing of election campaigns and political parties. See also CCPR/C/HND/CO/2, para. 45.

[213] Human Rights Committee, general comment No. 25 (1996), para. 19; and CCPR/C/GNQ/CO/1, paras. 58–59 (the main party apparently received public funds while opposition parties had to raise their own funds). See also A/HRC/21/63, para. 71 (use of State resources and neutrality during the election campaign); and A/HRC/20/27/Add.2, para. 90 (d) (equitable access to State resources for election campaigning).

IV. OTHER HUMAN RIGHTS CONSIDERATIONS FOR ELECTORAL PROCESSES

108. This chapter explores other human rights considerations that should be taken into account when designing and implementing electoral legal frameworks. However, it is not intended to be exhaustive or to provide technical guidance on the specific aspects of elections mentioned below.

A. Respect for relevant human rights norms and standards

109. Respect for a wide range of prerequisite human rights, as enumerated in the relevant human rights instruments (see chap. III above) is crucial to the conduct of free and genuine elections. Guarantees of free speech, opinion, information, assembly, association, movement, non-discrimination and the right to security of person take on particular significance in electoral processes. The prevailing atmosphere of an election period should be one of respect for human rights[214] and be characterized by an absence of intimidating factors and violence.

110. Laws in force that might have the effect of discouraging political participation should be repealed or amended, as should emergency or other exceptional legislation that unduly restricts fundamental rights. As mentioned above, international human rights law recognizes certain limitations on rights, such as freedom of movement, expression or peaceful assembly, may be permissible in times of public emergency, so long as they meet the requirements of legality, necessity, proportionality and non-discrimination. The Human Rights Committee has stated that, during states of emergency, any measures derogating from the Covenant are to be limited to the extent strictly required by the exigencies of the situation[215] and should not be calculated to corrupt or unnecessarily delay the electoral process. For example, the Human Rights Committee has stated that prohibiting, under a state of emergency, any kind of political dissent and depriving political opponents of any political right for a period as long as 15 years are not compatible with article 25 of the Covenant.[216]

[214] Guidelines for States on the effective implementation of the right to participate in public affairs, paras. 14–18, and the corresponding recommendations.

[215] Human Rights Committee, general comment No. 29 (2001), para. 4.

[216] *Silva et al. v. Uruguay*, paras. 8.4–9.

111. Guarantees for the fundamental right of periodic, free and genuine elections should be enshrined in the constitution or other high-level laws.[217] The legal authority for the prerequisite rights relevant in electoral processes – freedom of expression, opinion, information, peaceful assembly, association and movement and the right to non-discrimination, education and security of person – should also emanate from the highest law of the land.

112. Statutory language should be clear, concise, and adequately specific in order to ensure legal certainty and predictability[218] and avoid the potential for abuse of discretion or discriminatory application or impingement upon the rights of free expression or full participation. The legal framework for elections should also encourage participation by women, be available in minority languages[219] and be accessible to all persons with disabilities.[220]

113. Finally, States should develop an effective legal framework for the exercise of electoral rights in accordance with international human rights law and through an inclusive, transparent and participatory process to strengthen its acceptance and legitimacy.[221] This includes respect for the principles of legal certainty and predictability. Participation by civil society may ensure that the impact of all legislative options on specific groups is considered and may enhance ownership of these rules by all members of society.[222] This can, in turn, reduce disputes about electoral frameworks and procedures, and limit and reduce tensions and the potential for electoral violence.

B. Electoral management bodies

114. While universal human rights instruments do not expressly refer to electoral management bodies, the obligation for them to implement an electoral process that respects human rights can be derived from the general obligation imposed on the State to respect, protect and fulfil human rights, which is applicable to all its branches of government and offices.[223] Electoral management bodies may

---

[217] Human Rights Committee, general comment No. 25 (1996), para. 5.

[218] CERD/C/62/CO/1, para. 14 ("the Committee notes with concern that the misinterpretation of election laws has given rise to tensions between ethnic and religious groups").

[219] Human Rights Committee, general comment No. 25 (1996), para. 12. See also CCPR/C/CYP/CO/4, para. 22.

[220] CRPD/C/PER/CO/1, para. 45.

[221] Guidelines for States on the effective implementation of the right to participate in public affairs, para. 30.

[222] Ibid., para. 2.

[223] Human Rights Committee, general comment No. 31 (2004), para. 4.

vary in their structure and size. There are a number of models for such bodies – independent, governmental and mixed – any of which may be appropriate for a particular country, depending on many factors, including the individual circumstances and needs of the country at the time. Regardless of which model is adopted, electoral management bodies are expected to ensure the integrity of the electoral process. Where an electoral authority is established, the Human Rights Committee has recommended that it should ensure that the electoral process "is conducted fairly, impartially and in accordance with established laws which are compatible with the Covenant".[224] Electoral management bodies should be able to function independently[225] (in the sense that they should not bend to governmental, political or other partisan influence in their decisions), impartially and in a gender-sensitive manner,[226] irrespective of their composition. Such bodies should be open, transparent and maximally consultative in their decision-making and provide access to relevant information for all stakeholders.[227]

115. Legal guarantees should be in place to insulate the electoral administration from bias or corruption.[228] Electoral activities, including the decision-making process, should be conducted in a wholly transparent and inclusive manner.[229]

116. International human rights standards should also be applied in relation to the labour rights of election officials. Safe and healthy working conditions should be guaranteed in electoral contexts, including for poll workers.[230]

C. Constituency/boundary delimitation

117. The process of identification of electoral districts and boundaries should respect the international norm of equal suffrage. As stated by the Human Rights Committee, "the principle of one person, one vote must apply, and within the framework of each State's electoral system, the vote of one elector

224 Human Rights Committee, general comment No. 25 (1996), para. 20.

225 Ibid.; CCPR/C/TJK/CO/3, para. 55 (e) (ensure the full independence of the electoral commission); and CCPR/C/MDG/CO/4, para. 54 (strengthen the independence of the electoral commission).

226 UN-Women and UNDP, *Inclusive Electoral Processes: A Guide for Electoral Management Bodies on Promoting Gender Equality and Women's Participation* (2015).

227 Guidelines for States on the effective implementation of the right to participate in public affairs, para. 45.

228 United Nations Convention against Corruption, arts. 5 and 7. See also CCPR/C/CMR/CO/5 ("the State party should take the necessary steps to guarantee the independence of [the electoral oversight body]"), para. 44.

229 Guidelines for States on the effective implementation of the right to participate in public affairs, paras. 2 and 30.

230 Article 7 (b) of the International Covenant on Economic, Social and Cultural Rights guarantees safe and healthy working conditions.

should be equal to the vote of another."[231] The drawing of electoral boundaries and the method of allocating votes should not distort the distribution of voters, discriminate against any group or exclude or restrict unreasonably the right of citizens to choose their representatives freely.[232] The treaty bodies have expressed concern about electoral boundaries being disproportionately imbalanced in favour of certain geographic areas.[233]

118. Constituency delimitation procedures should take into account a range of information, including available census data, territorial integrity, geographical distribution, topography, etc.

D. Voter registration

119. The Human Rights Committee has observed that "States must take effective measures to ensure that all persons entitled to vote are able to exercise that right."[234] This is in line with the principle of universal suffrage outlined in chapter III, section B.2 above. If advance registration of voters is implemented, any overly restrictive obstacles to such registration should not be imposed. The Committee has also noted that "if residence requirements apply to registration, they must be reasonable".[235] If no registration is required in advance of polling, it is important to implement alternative measures for preventing double-voting (e.g. the use of indelible ink) and voting by ineligible persons. Adequate time should be allocated for voter registration so as to provide the greatest opportunity for voters to register.

120. Registration procedures should accommodate broad participation of eligible voters. As stated in chapter II, any suspension or exclusion of participatory rights is prohibited except on grounds that are established by law and are objective and reasonable.[236] For example, the Human Rights Committee has clarified that "if conviction for an offence is a basis for suspending the right to vote or to stand for office, such restriction must be proportionate to the offence and the

---

[231] Human Rights Committee, general comment No. 25 (1996), para. 21.

[232] Ibid. See also *Mátyus v. Slovakia*, paras. 9.2–10 (in which the Committee concluded that the State party had violated article 25 (a) and (c) by drawing election districts with substantial differences between the number of inhabitants or registered voters for each elected representative).

[233] CCPR/C/MDG/CO/4, para. 53 (the electoral map did not guarantee equality among districts); and CERD/C/JOR/CO/13-17, para. 13.

[234] Human Rights Committee, general comment No. 25 (1996), para. 11.

[235] Ibid.

[236] Ibid., para. 4.

sentence".[237] Therefore, States should not impose automatic blanket bans on the right to vote for persons serving or having completed a custodial sentence that do not take into account the nature and gravity of the criminal offence or the length of the sentence.[238] Furthermore, persons who are deprived of liberty but who have not been convicted should not be excluded from exercising the right to vote.[239] Other unreasonable barriers to voter registration should be removed, including onerous, burdensome or culturally inadequate administrative requirements for accessing the necessary documentation to exercise the right to vote, especially for women, minorities, indigenous peoples, those living in remote areas and internally displaced persons.[240] Where needed, special measures should be taken to increase the representation of women,[241] minorities[242] and persons with disabilities as voters on the register. With regard to this latter issue, national legal provisions that limit the right to vote on grounds of legal capacity should be revoked and legal measures should be adopted to ensure that all persons with disabilities, especially those with intellectual or psychosocial disabilities, may exercise their right to vote (see chap. III).[243] Regarding age limitations, the Human Rights Committee considers that the right to vote should be available to every adult citizen.[244]

121. Where relevant, attention should be paid to the digitalization of voter registration and any potential risks to human rights derived therefrom. For example, voter registration databases maintained by government authorities may be susceptible to hacking and other malicious attacks. Such data breaches not only interfere with individuals' right to privacy, but may also have an impact on freedom of expression and public confidence in the integrity of the electoral process. The Special

---

[237] *Arias Leiva v. Colombia* (CCPR/C/123/D/2537/2015), para. 11.6.

[238] Guidelines for States on the effective implementation of the right to participate in public affairs, para. 42. See also CCPR/C/EST/CO/4, para. 34; and CCPR/C/TKM/CO/2, para. 51.

[239] Human Rights Committee, general comment No. 25 (1996), para. 14. See also *Gorji-Dinka v. Cameroon* (CCPR/C/83/D/1134/2002), para. 5.6.

[240] Guidelines for States on the effective implementation of the right to participate in public affairs, para. 36. See also Human Rights Committee, general comment No. 25 (1996), para. 11.

[241] See, inter alia, CEDAW/C/GUA/CO/7, para. 26; CCPR/C/SLV/CO/7, para. 12; and CCPR/C/LBN/CO/3, para. 18. See also A/57/38(SUPP), paras. 402–403, on the low rate of registration of women as voters and their low representation on electoral lists in Yemen.

[242] CCPR/C/BIH/CO/3, para. 12; CCPR/C/ALB/CO/2, para. 23 (e), on ensuring that all Roma have identity cards so as to facilitate their right to vote; CCPR/C/HUN/CO/5, para. 21 ("the State party should adopt measures to address the shortcomings of the minority election register"); and CERD/C/IND/CO/19, para. 17 ("many Dalits are not included in electoral rolls or otherwise denied the right to vote").

[243] See, inter alia, CCPR/C/LTU/CO/4, para. 14; CCPR/C/GTM/CO/4, para. 27; and CCPR/C/AUS/CO/6, para. 48. See also *Bujdosó et al. v. Hungary*, para. 9.4; CRPD/C/PER/CO/1, para. 45; and guidelines for States on the effective implementation of the right to participate in public affairs, para. 38.

[244] Human Rights Committee, general comment No. 25 (1996), para. 4.

Rapporteur on the promotion and protection of the right to freedom of opinion and expression has stated that such cases would "engage the State's obligation to conduct appropriate investigations and provide effective remedies".[245]

E. Parties, nominations and candidates

122. In their internal management, political parties should respect the applicable provisions of article 25 in order to enable citizens to exercise their rights thereunder.[246] It is important that legal provisions concerning candidate qualifications be clear and promote the participation of the full diversity of the population and that, at a minimum, the electoral legal framework be non-discriminatory. The right to stand for election may only be subject to restrictions that are objective, reasonable and non-discriminatory, such as a minimum age.[247] This is necessary to ensure that persons entitled to vote have a free choice of candidates (see chap. III).[248] Persons who are otherwise eligible to stand for election should not be excluded by unreasonable or discriminatory requirements, such as education, residence or descent, or by reason of political affiliation.[249] Any disqualifications should be subject to effective and independent complaints and appeals procedures.[250] Equal conditions should be ensured for independent candidates to stand for elections[251] and unreasonable requirements should not be imposed on their candidacies.[252] Moreover, persons should not suffer from discrimination or disadvantage of any kind because of their candidacy.[253]

---

[245] Special Rapporteur on the promotion and protection of the right to freedom of opinion and expression, "Freedom of expression and elections in the digital age", p. 13.

[246] Human Rights Committee, general comment No. 25 (1996), para. 26.

[247] Ibid., para. 15. See also *Delgado Burgos v. Plurinational State of Bolivia*, para. 11.5; *Nasheed v. Maldives*, para. 8.6; *Paksas v. Lithuania*, para. 8.4; *Narrain et al. v. Mauritius* (CCPR/C/105/D/1744/2007), para. 15.5; *Sudalenko v. Belarus*, para. 6.5; CCPR/C/TJK/CO/3, paras. 54–55 (a), (undue limitations based on language, education and residency requirements); and CCPR/C/BIH/CO/2, para. 6 (exclusion from standing for election based on ethnicity).

[248] Human Rights Committee, general comment No. 25 (1996), para. 15.

[249] Ibid.

[250] *Sinitsin v. Belarus* (CCPR/C/88/D/1047/2002), para. 7.3 (no effective remedies available to challenge the ruling declaring his nomination invalid).

[251] Human Rights Committee, general comment No. 25 (1996), para. 17; and CCPR/C/RWA/CO/3, para. 21.

[252] Guidelines for States on the effective implementation of the right to participate in public affairs, para. 35. See also *Ignatane v. Latvia*, para. 7.5. (in which the author was struck off the list of candidates on the basis of insufficient proficiency in the official language).

[253] Human Rights Committee, general comment No. 25 (1996), para. 15. See also CCPR/C/COD/CO/4, para. 48 (intimidation of opponents and candidates in the presidential election); and CCPR/C/AZE/CO/4, para. 43 (criminal law provisions used to exclude opposition candidates from electoral processes).

123. Candidates should not face unreasonable restrictions on participation[254] or campaigning, including with regard to their rights to freedom of expression,[255] assembly and association.[256] Political candidates' freedom of movement[257] and right to security[258] should also be guaranteed. As political parties constitute a subset of associations,[259] their members' freedom of association should also be ensured in the context of elections. Procedures for nomination of candidates, registration of party agents and campaign financing[260] should be clearly established by the electoral legal framework. In addition, the electoral calendar should provide adequate time for campaigning and public information efforts. Candidates should be able to challenge a refusal to accept their nominations before a competent tribunal.[261]

124. In situations in which women are underrepresented, States should take proactive measures through electoral legislation to increase their participation, such as the adoption of temporary special measures, including quotas for women, targeted recruitment, financial assistance, outreach, training of women candidates and provision of additional security for women (see chap. III).[262] Regarding persons under guardianship or otherwise lacking legal capacity, as in the case of the exercise of the right to vote, the Committee on the Rights of Persons with Disabilities has recalled that "a person's decision-making ability cannot be a justification for any exclusion of persons with disabilities from exercising their political rights", including the right to stand for election.[263] In terms of age restrictions, while it may be reasonable to require a higher age

---

254 CCPR/C/TKM/CO/2, paras. 48–49 (excessive restrictions on the establishment and functioning of political parties).

255 Human Rights Committee, general comment No. 34 (2011), para. 37. See also *Korneenko v. Belarus* (CCPR/C/95/D/1553/2007), paras. 8.3–8.4; and CCPR/C/JPN/CO/5, para. 26 (prohibition of door-to-door canvassing and restrictions on written materials that may be distributed during pre-election campaigns).

256 A/68/299, para. 6.

257 CCPR/CO/80/UGA, para. 22 (restrictions on freedom of movement of political opponents).

258 CCPR/C/NGA/CO/2, paras. 48–49 (ensure protection from violence and threats); and CCPR/CO/80/COL, para. 11 (arrest of election candidates).

259 A/68/299, para. 30. See also A/HRC/20/27, paras. 51–52.

260 CCPR/C/HND/CO/2, para. 45.

261 International Covenant on Civil and Political Rights, art. 2 (3) (a).

262 CCPR/C/BEN/CO/2, para. 10–11; CEDAW/C/AUT/CO/9, paras. 26–27; CEDAW/C/CIV/CO/4, paras. 33–34; and CEDAW/C/COL/CO/9, para. 30 (a). See also A/HRC/23/50, paras. 96–97; and guidelines for States on the effective implementation of the right to participate in public affairs, para. 31.

263 Committee on the Rights of Persons with Disabilities, general comment No. 1 (2014), para. 48; and *Bujdosó et al. v. Hungary*, para. 9.4 (exclusion of the right to vote).

for election or appointment to particular offices than for exercising the right to vote,[264] some States have started aligning the minimum voting age and the minimum age of eligibility to stand for elections, to encourage the political participation of young persons.[265] In addition, electoral laws and procedures should ensure a level playing field and treat all political actors, including opposition parties, on an equal basis.[266]

F. Voting operations

125. The way in which a country conducts voting operations and the degree to which they are transparent are crucial in ensuring the enjoyment of relevant human rights, in addition to increasing public trust in the process and the results. Voting operations should protect the process from fraudulent practices, and "the security of ballot boxes must be guaranteed".[267] Specific concerns have arisen with the digitalization of electoral processes and in particular electronic voting, that is the use of electronic means to cast and count the votes. While the use of digital technologies for voting operations has the potential to increase participation, reduce irregularities and strengthen public trust, introducing new technologies in elections is complex and should be a gradual process that is able to clarify the problem to be resolved through any new technology and takes time to consider the technical, financial and political feasibility of the innovation through broad consultation.[268]

126. As mentioned in chapter III, electoral and voting materials, including digital ones, should be published in the various national and minority languages and be accessible to persons with disabilities.[269] Voters with specific needs for support, including persons with disabilities,[270] older persons, conscripts, migrant workers

---

264 Human Rights Committee, general comment No. 25 (1996), para. 4.

265 Guidelines for States on the effective implementation of the right to participate in public affairs, para. 40. See also A/HRC/34/46, para. 39.

266 CCPR/C/RWA/CO/3, para. 21; A/HRC/20/27/Add.2, para. 90 (d) (ensure equal access to State resources for campaigning); and A/HRC/21/63, paras. 62 (ensure level playing field) and 71 (use of government resources).

267 Human Rights Committee, general comment No. 25 (1996), para. 20.

268 A/74/285, para. 38.

269 Human Rights Committee, general comment No. 25 (1996), para. 12; and CCPR/C/BGR/CO/4, paras. 35–36 (voting material in one language only, discrimination against minorities). See also guidelines for States on the effective implementation of the right to participate in public affairs, para. 39 (d).

270 CCPR/C/MLT/CO/2, para. 21 (blind persons and persons with visual impairments being denied or prevented from exercising their right to vote by secret ballots); and CCPR/C/PRY/CO/3, para. 11 (access to voting stations and voting slips). See also CRPD/C/ARG/CO/1, paras. 47–48 (access to the polls for institutionalized persons with disabilities); and CRPD/C/PER/CO/1, paras. 44–45 (same issue).

out of the country,[271] foreign service personnel and prisoners who have retained voting rights, should be provided with reasonable accommodation. Potential legislative and practical obstacles for women voters should be detected and addressed. Positive measures should be taken to overcome specific difficulties, such as illiteracy, language barriers, poverty or impediments to freedom of movement that prevent persons entitled to vote from exercising their right effectively.[272] Based on the principle of universal suffrage and non-discrimination in the exercise of the right to vote, it is important that polling stations be geographically distributed so as to enable equitable access within each constituency.

127. Complaints and appeals mechanisms and appropriate audit procedures should be available and all electoral activities should be open to observers, party/candidate agents and media (see chap. III and chap. IV, sect. G, on electoral justice). Enabling the presence of observers, party/candidate agents and media and their access to electoral processes at all times (while respecting individual secrecy and privacy) ensures transparency of the process.[273] Counting should be transparent[274] and open to official observation by concerned parties.[275] Considering the impact that vote counting, verification, reporting of results and retention of official materials may have on the free expression of the will of the electors, it is essential that these operations be secure and transparent. Appropriate audit procedures should be available in case of questionable results.[276] Finally, the Human Rights Committee has recommended an "independent scrutiny of the voting and counting process",[277] which can contribute to public confidence in, and acceptance of, the outcome of polling.

G. Electoral justice

128. In accordance with the right to a fair trial (International Covenant on Civil and Political Rights, art. 14) and the right to an effective remedy (ibid., art. 2 (3)), the right to challenge election results and for aggrieved parties to

---

[271] International Convention on the Protection of the Rights of All Migrant Workers and Members of Their Families, art. 41. See also CMW/C/ALB/CO/2, paras. 55–56; CMW/C/ECU/CO/3, paras. 36–37; CMW/C/BGD/CO/1, paras. 43–44; and CMW/C/NGA/CO/1, paras. 43–44.

[272] Human Rights Committee, general comment No. 25 (1996), para. 12.

[273] Ibid., para. 20. See also CCPR/C/IRN/CO/3, para. 29. See also guidelines for States on the effective implementation of the right to participate in public affairs, para. 44.

[274] CCPR/C/BLR/CO/5, para. 57.

[275] Human Rights Committee, general comment No. 25 (1996), para. 20; and CCPR/C/HND/CO/2, para. 45.

[276] *Katashynskyi v. Ukraine*, para. 7.2 (lost ballots and no re-count ordered).

[277] Human Rights Committee, general comment No. 25 (1996), para. 20.

seek redress should be available and provided by law (see chap. III).[278] Access to an independent judicial review or other complaints and appeals processes and audit procedures should be provided so that electors have confidence in the electoral process.[279]

129. Legal frameworks should set out the scope of available review procedures and the powers of the independent and impartial judicial body charged with such review. Multiple levels of review, where available, should also be clearly determined in legislation. Electoral laws should also provide remedies that are prompt, adequate and effective and enforceable within the context of the electoral calendar.[280] Persons with disabilities should be provided with procedural accommodation to ensure access to justice (Convention on the Rights of Persons with Disabilities, art. 13). Women's access to justice should also be ensured,[281] as well as for other marginalized groups.

H. Offences, penalties and maintenance of order

130. The national legal framework and policies should protect the electoral process from coercion, corruption, official malfeasance, obstruction, intimidation and all other forms of abusive interference and violence, including sexual violence.[282] Prosecutions, procedures and penalties should respect international standards for human rights in the administration of justice.[283]

131. Decisions regarding the maintenance of peace and order at polling stations should be made by balancing concern for security against the potential intimidating effect of a police, security or military presence and should be gender-sensitive. Such decisions should be consistent with human dignity and the human rights

[278] Ibid. and Human Rights Committee, general comment No. 31 (2004), para. 15. See also *Delgado Burgoa v. Plurinational State of Bolivia*, para. 13; and *Sinitsin v. Belarus*, para. 7.3. See also CCPR/C/LBR/CO/1, paras. 44–45.

[279] Human Rights Committee, general comment No. 25 (1996), para. 20; and *Katashynskyi v. Ukraine*, para. 7.2 (lack of access to an independent judicial review).

[280] Guidelines for States on the effective implementation of the right to participate in public affairs, para. 46.

[281] Committee on the Elimination of Discrimination against Women, general recommendation No. 33 (2015).

[282] Human Rights Committee, general comment No. 25 (1996), para. 11. See also A/HRC/14/24/Add.7, para. 90.

[283] See OHCHR, *Human Rights in the Administration of Justice: A Facilitator's Guide on Human Rights for Judges, Prosecutors and Lawyers*, Professional Training Series No. 9/Add.1 (New York and Geneva, 2011).

of all persons.[284] Civil and criminal liability should be imposed for acts of misfeasance, nonfeasance and malfeasance by election officials.

132. In the particular case of compulsory voting systems, the Human Rights Committee has considered that "any sanction for the failure to vote must be established by law, reasonable and proportionate and must not affect the enjoyment or exercise of the rights under the Covenant".[285]

I. Media: access and regulation

133. Fair media access by all political candidates and parties for campaigning and advertising purposes is also important.[286] Fair media access may be even more important in situations in which the major information media are controlled by the Government. Media regulations should provide for safeguards against political censorship, unfair government advantage and unequal/unequitable access during the campaign period.[287] Women and men candidates should receive equal visibility in the public media during election campaigns.[288]

134. As stated by the Special Rapporteur on the promotion and protection of the right to freedom of opinion and expression, in situations in which media are State owned, national legal frameworks should ensure that all political parties have access to them and are treated fairly and equitably. When paid political advertising is allowed, private media outlets should be required to charge all parties and candidates the same rates without discrimination. The incumbent Government or candidates should not be given preferential or disproportionately extensive media coverage.[289]

135. Furthermore, the rapid expansion of the digital space has created multiple alternative channels of communication and social media in particular has become a key source of information with new concerns emerging, including disinformation and big data manipulation.[290]

---

284 Code of Conduct for Law Enforcement Officials, art. 2.

285 *Alger v. Australia* (CCPR/C/120/D/2237/2013), para. 7.3.

286 A/HRC/26/30, para. 48. See also Special Rapporteur on the promotion and protection of the right to freedom of opinion and expression, "Freedom of expression and elections in the digital age", p. 4.

287 CCPR/C/TJK/CO/3, para. 55 (f); CCPR/C/GNQ/CO/1, paras. 58–59; and CCPR/C/KWT/CO/3, paras. 40–41.

288 CEDAW/C/CHE/CO/3, paras. 33–34.

289 A/HRC/26/30, para. 58.

290 See the textbox on the impact of big data manipulation and social media on elections above.

136. Fair media access implies not only equality regarding the allocation of time and space, but also attention to the hour of broadcasting (i.e. prime time versus late broadcasting) and the placement of printed advertisements (i.e. front page versus back page).[291] The Special Rapporteur on the promotion and protection of the right to freedom of opinion and expression has recommended that the media be encouraged to put in place mechanisms to ensure that all media actors adhere to the highest ethical standards of objective reporting, and guarantee equal coverage of political parties in a way that facilitates broad voter education and ensures all parties across the political spectrum are heard.[292] Training for journalists and other media workers should also be promoted in order to challenge gender stereotyping and misrepresentation of women in the media[293] and to ensure equal coverage of women and men candidates.

137. A valuable mechanism for ensuring fair and responsible broadcasting during election periods may be an independent body charged with monitoring political broadcasts and the allocation of time to various political parties and candidates, and receiving and acting upon complaints regarding media access, fairness and responsibility. Alternatively, these functions may be discharged by several different institutions, depending on the context.

138. As noted by the Special Rapporteur on the promotion and protection of the right to freedom of opinion and expression, "transparency of media ownership enables readers, viewers and voters to understand the structures of influence that underpin the campaign, advertising and editorial content that so often determine their political choices. States should find a way, either through regulatory policy or industry-led self-regulation processes, to promote greater transparency in media ownership and influence. ... However, the requirement for transparency of private media ownership should not be used as a means of de facto media licensing."[294]

139. Securing responsible and gender-sensitive electoral broadcasting and publication in the media can, in part, be served by agreement on a code of conduct for the media. According to the Special Rapporteur on the promotion and protection of the right to freedom of opinion and expression, self-regulation

---

[291] Guidelines for States on the effective implementation of the right to participate in public affairs, para. 34.
[292] A/HRC/26/30, para. 57.
[293] Guidelines for States on the effective implementation of the right to participate in public affairs, para. 33.
[294] A/HRC/26/30, para. 67.

is arguably the most effective means of ensuring that the media live up to their own ethical standards while remaining free from the influence of the State.[295] Regulatory systems should take into account the differences between the print and broadcast sectors and the Internet, while also noting the manner in which various media converge.[296]

J. Public information and voter education

140. Voter education, including through media education and digital literacy programmes, is essential to ensure the effective exercise of the right to vote by an informed community (see chap. III on the right to education).[297] Voters need to be confident in the integrity of the electoral process and their right to participate in it. Funding and administration should be provided for objective, non-partisan voter education and information campaigns. It is important that all civic education programmes be inclusive and target individuals and groups that are marginalized or discriminated against.[298] Voter education is especially critical for populations with little or no experience of democratic elections, for example young persons who vote for the first time. The public should be well informed as to why voting is important, as well as where, when and how to vote. Voter education campaigns should extend throughout the territory of the country, including to rural and outlying areas.

141. Materials should be widely available to ensure the meaningful participation of all eligible voters. Electoral and voting materials should be published in the various national languages, including minority languages and be accessible to persons with disabilities.[299] Specific methods, such as photographs and symbols, should be adopted to take into account various levels of literacy.[300] Voter education and training should also target equality between men and women.[301]

---

[295] Ibid., para. 56.

[296] Human Rights Committee, general comment No. 34 (2011), para. 39.

[297] Human Rights Committee, general comment No. 25 (1996), para. 11.

[298] Guidelines for States on the effective implementation of the right to participate in public affairs, para. 24.

[299] Human Rights Committee, general comment No. 25 (1996), para. 12. See also guidelines for States on the effective implementation of the right to participate in public affairs, para. 39 (d).

[300] Human Rights Committee, general comment No. 25 (1996), para. 12.

[301] Committee on the Elimination of Discrimination against Women, general recommendations No. 3 (1987) and 19 (1992); CEDAW/C/IRL/CO/6-7, para. 35 (b); and CEDAW/C/ETH/CO/6-7, para. 27.

ANNEX I
NORMS AND STANDARDS IN INTERNATIONAL HUMAN RIGHTS INSTRUMENTS RELEVANT TO ELECTIONS AND POLITICAL PARTICIPATION

A. Right to political participation

Declaration on the Right and Responsibility of Individuals, Groups and Organs of Society to Promote and Protect Universally Recognized Human Rights and Fundamental Freedoms

Article 8

1. Everyone has the right, individually and in association with others, to have effective access, on a non-discriminatory basis, to participation in the government of his or her country and in the conduct of public affairs.
2. This includes, inter alia, the right, individually and in association with others, to submit to governmental bodies and agencies and organizations concerned with public affairs criticism and proposals for improving their functioning and to draw attention to any aspect of their work that may hinder or impede the promotion, protection and realization of human rights and fundamental freedoms.

Convention on the Rights of the Child

Article 15

1. States Parties recognize the rights of the child to freedom of association and to freedom of peaceful assembly.
2. No restrictions may be placed on the exercise of these rights other than those imposed in conformity with the law and which are necessary in a democratic society in the interests of national security or public safety, public order (*ordre public*), the protection of public health or morals or the protection of the rights and freedoms of others.

Declaration on the Right to Development

Article 1

1. The right to development is an inalienable human right by virtue of which every human person and all peoples are entitled to participate in, contribute to, and enjoy economic, social, cultural and political development, in which all human rights and fundamental freedoms can be fully realized.

...

Article 2

1. The human person is the central subject of development and should be the active participant and beneficiary of the right to development.

2. All human beings have a responsibility for development, individually and collectively, taking into account the need for full respect for their human rights and fundamental freedoms as well as their duties to the community, which alone can ensure the free and complete fulfilment of the human being, and they should therefore promote and protect an appropriate political, social and economic order for development.

3. States have the right and the duty to formulate appropriate national development policies that aim at the constant improvement of the well-being of the entire population and of all individuals, on the basis of their active, free and meaningful participation in development and in the fair distribution of the benefits resulting therefrom.

Article 8

...

2. States should encourage popular participation in all spheres as an important factor in development and in the full realization of all human rights.

International Covenant on Economic, Social and Cultural Rights

Article 8

1. The States Parties to the present Covenant undertake to ensure:

   (a) The right of everyone to form trade unions and join the trade union of his choice, subject only to the rules of the organization concerned, for the promotion and protection of his economic and social interests. No restrictions may be placed on the exercise of this right other than those prescribed by law and which are necessary in a democratic society in the interests of national security or public order or for the protection of the rights and freedoms of others;

   (b) The right of trade unions to establish national federations or confederations and the right of the latter to form or join international trade-union organizations;

(c) The right of trade unions to function freely subject to no limitations other than those prescribed by law and which are necessary in a democratic society in the interests of national security or public order or for the protection of the rights and freedoms of others;

(d) The right to strike, provided that it is exercised in conformity with the laws of the particular country.

2. This article shall not prevent the imposition of lawful restrictions on the exercise of these rights by members of the armed forces or of the police or of the administration of the State.

3. Nothing in this article shall authorize States Parties to the International Labour Organisation Convention of 1948 concerning Freedom of Association and Protection of the Right to Organize to take legislative measures which would prejudice, or apply the law in such a manner as would prejudice, the guarantees provided for in that Convention.

International Covenant on Civil and Political Rights

Article 25

Every citizen shall have the right and the opportunity, without any of the distinctions mentioned in article 2 and without unreasonable restrictions:

(a) To take part in the conduct of public affairs, directly or through freely chosen representatives;

(b) To vote and to be elected at genuine periodic elections which shall be by universal and equal suffrage and shall be held by secret ballot, guaranteeing the free expression of the will of the electors;

(c) To have access, on general terms of equality, to public service in his country.

Universal Declaration of Human Rights

Article 21

1. Everyone has the right to take part in the government of his country, directly or through freely chosen representatives.

2. Everyone has the right of equal access to public service in his country.

3. The will of the people shall be the basis of the authority of government; this will shall be expressed in periodic and genuine elections which shall be by universal and equal suffrage and shall be held by secret vote or by equivalent free voting procedures.

B. Non-discrimination and equal access to political participation

United Nations Declaration on the Rights of Indigenous Peoples

Article 5

Indigenous peoples have the right to maintain and strengthen their distinct political, legal, economic, social and cultural institutions, while retaining their right to participate fully, if they so choose, in the political, economic, social and cultural life of the State.

Article 18

Indigenous peoples have the right to participate in decision-making in matters which would affect their rights, through representatives chosen by themselves in accordance with their own procedures, as well as to maintain and develop their own indigenous decision-making institutions.

Convention on the Rights of Persons with Disabilities

Article 29 – Participation in political and public life

States Parties shall guarantee to persons with disabilities political rights and the opportunity to enjoy them on an equal basis with others, and shall undertake:

(a) To ensure that persons with disabilities can effectively and fully participate in political and public life on an equal basis with others, directly or through freely chosen representatives, including the right and opportunity for persons with disabilities to vote and be elected, inter alia, by:

(i) Ensuring that voting procedures, facilities and materials are appropriate, accessible and easy to understand and use;

(ii) Protecting the right of persons with disabilities to vote by secret ballot in elections and public referendums without intimidation, and to stand for elections, to effectively hold office and perform all public functions at all levels of government, facilitating the use of assistive and new technologies where appropriate;

(iii) Guaranteeing the free expression of the will of persons with disabilities as electors and to this end, where necessary, at their request, allowing assistance in voting by a person of their own choice;

(b) To promote actively an environment in which persons with disabilities can effectively and fully participate in the conduct of public affairs, without discrimination and on an equal basis with others, and encourage their participation in public affairs, including:

(i) Participation in non-governmental organizations and associations concerned with the public and political life of the country, and in the activities and administration of political parties;

(ii) Forming and joining organizations of persons with disabilities to represent persons with disabilities at international, national, regional and local levels.

Durban Declaration and Programme of Action

22. *Requests* States:

...

(d) To consult indigenous representatives in the process of decision-making concerning policies and measures that directly affect them.

Declaration on the Rights of Persons Belonging to National or Ethnic, Religious and Linguistic Minorities

Article 2

...

2. Persons belonging to minorities have the right to participate effectively in cultural, religious, social, economic and public life.

...

International Convention on the Protection of All Migrant Workers and Members of Their Families

Article 41

1. Migrant workers and members of their families shall have the right to participate in public affairs of their State of origin and to vote and to be elected at elections of that State, in accordance with its legislation.
2. The States concerned shall, as appropriate and in accordance with their legislation, facilitate the exercise of these rights.

Article 42

1. States Parties shall consider the establishment of procedures or institutions through which account may be taken, both in States of origin and in States of employment, of special needs, aspirations and obligations of migrant workers and of their families and shall envisage, as appropriate, the possibility for migrant workers and members of their families to have their freely chosen representatives in those institutions.
2. States of employment shall facilitate, in accordance with their national legislation, the consultation or participation of migrant workers and members of their families in decisions concerning the life and administration of local communities.
3. Migrant workers may enjoy political rights in the State of employment if that State, in the exercise of its sovereignty, grants them such rights.

Convention on the Rights of the Child

Article 12

1. States Parties shall assure to the child who is capable of forming his or her own views the right to express those views freely in all matters affecting the child, the views of the child being given due weight in accordance with the age and maturity of the child.

...

Convention on the Elimination of All Forms of Discrimination against Women

Article 7

States Parties shall take all appropriate measures to eliminate discrimination against women in the political and public life of the country and, in particular, shall ensure to women, on equal terms with men, the right:

(a) To vote in all elections and public referenda and to be eligible for election to all publicly elected bodies;

(b) To participate in the formulation of government policy and the implementation thereof and to hold public office and perform all public functions at all levels of government;

(c) To participate in non-governmental organizations and associations concerned with the public and political life of the country.

International Covenant on Civil and Political Rights

Article 2

1. Each State Party to the present Covenant undertakes to respect and to ensure to all individuals within its territory and subject to its jurisdiction the rights recognized in the present Covenant, without distinction of any kind, such as race, colour, sex, language, religion, political or other opinion, national or social origin, property, birth or other status.

...

Article 3

The States Parties to the present Covenant undertake to ensure the equal right of men and women to the enjoyment of all civil and political rights set forth in the present Covenant.

Article 26

All persons are equal before the law and are entitled without any discrimination to the equal protection of the law. In this respect, the law shall prohibit any discrimination and guarantee to all persons equal and effective protection against discrimination on any ground such as race, colour, sex, language, religion, political or other opinion, national or social origin, property, birth or other status.

International Convention on the Elimination of All Forms of Racial Discrimination

Article 5

In compliance with the fundamental obligations laid down in article 2 of this Convention, States Parties undertake to prohibit and to eliminate racial discrimination in all its forms and to guarantee the right of everyone, without distinction as to race, colour, or national or ethnic origin, to equality before the law, notably in the enjoyment of the following rights:

...

(c) Political rights, in particular the right to participate in elections – to vote and to stand for election – on the basis of universal and equal suffrage, to take part in the Government as well as in the conduct of public affairs at any level and to have equal access to public service;

...

Convention on the Political Rights of Women

Article I

Women shall be entitled to vote in all elections on equal terms with men, without discrimination.

Article II

Women shall be eligible for election to all publicly elected bodies, established by national law, on equal terms with men, without any discrimination.

Article III

Women shall be entitled to hold public office and to exercise all public functions, established by national law, on equal terms with men, without any discrimination.

Universal Declaration of Human Rights

Article 2

Everyone is entitled to all the rights and freedoms set forth in this Declaration, without distinction of any kind, such as race, colour, sex, language, religion, political or other opinion, national or social origin, property, birth or other status. Furthermore, no distinction shall be made on the basis of the political, jurisdictional or international status of the country or territory to which a person belongs, whether it be independent, trust, non-self-governing or under any other limitation of sovereignty.

Article 7

All are equal before the law and are entitled without any discrimination to equal protection of the law. All are entitled to equal protection against any discrimination in violation of this Declaration and against any incitement to such discrimination.

C. Right to self-determination

Declaration on the Granting of Independence to Colonial Countries and Peoples

2. All peoples have the right to self-determination; by virtue of that right they freely determine their political status and freely pursue their economic, social and cultural development.

5. Immediate steps shall be taken, in Trust and Non-Self-Governing Territories or all other territories which have not yet attained independence, to transfer all powers to the peoples of those territories, without any conditions or reservations, in accordance with their freely expressed will and desire, without any distinction as to race, creed or colour, in order to enable them to enjoy complete independence and freedom.

United Nations Declaration on the Rights of Indigenous Peoples

Article 3

Indigenous peoples have the right to self-determination. By virtue of that right they freely determine their political status and freely pursue their economic, social and cultural development.

Article 4

Indigenous peoples, in exercising their right to self-determination, have the right to autonomy or self-government in matters relating to their internal and local affairs, as well as ways and means for financing their autonomous functions.

Declaration on Principles of International Law concerning Friendly Relations and Cooperation among States in accordance with the Charter of the United Nations

1. *Solemnly proclaims* the following principles:

...

Every State has the duty to refrain from any forcible action which deprives peoples referred to in the elaboration of the principle of equal rights and self-determination of their right to self-determination and freedom and independence.

International Covenant on Civil and Political Rights and International Covenant on Economic, Social and Cultural Rights

Common article 1

1. All peoples have the right of self-determination. By virtue of that right they freely determine their political status and freely pursue their economic, social and cultural development.

...

Charter of the United Nations

Article 1

The Purposes of the United Nations are:

...

2. To develop friendly relations among nations based on respect for the principle of equal rights and self-determination of peoples, and to take other appropriate measures to strengthen universal peace;

3. To achieve international co-operation in solving international problems of an economic, social, cultural, or humanitarian character, and in promoting and encouraging respect for human rights and for fundamental freedoms for all without distinction as to race, sex, language, or religion;

...

Article 73

Members of the United Nations which have or assume responsibilities for the administration of territories whose peoples have not yet attained a full measure of self-government recognize the principle that the interests of the inhabitants of these territories are paramount, and accept as a sacred trust the obligation to promote to the utmost, within the system of international peace and security established by the present Charter, the well-being of the inhabitants of these territories, and, to this end:

...

(b) to develop self-government, to take due account of the political aspirations of the peoples, and to assist them in the progressive development of their free political institutions, according to the particular circumstances of each territory and its peoples and their varying stages of advancement;

...

Article 76

The basic objectives of the trusteeship system, in accordance with the Purposes of the United Nations laid down in Article 1 of the present Charter, shall be:

...

(b) to promote the political, economic, social, and educational advancement of the inhabitants of the trust territories, and their progressive development towards self-government or independence as may be appropriate to the particular circumstances of each territory and its peoples and the freely expressed wishes of the peoples concerned, and as may be provided by the terms of each trusteeship agreement;

(c) to encourage respect for human rights and for fundamental freedoms for all without distinction as to race, sex, language, or religion, and to encourage recognition of the interdependence of the peoples of the world;

...

ANNEX II
SELECTED REGIONAL INSTRUMENTS RELEVANT TO ELECTIONS AND POLITICAL PARTICIPATION

A. Right to political participation

Document of the Copenhagen Meeting of the Conference on the Human Dimension of the Conference on Security and Cooperation in Europe

7. To ensure that the will of the people serves as the basis of the authority of government, the participating States will

    7.1. hold free elections at reasonable intervals, as established by law;

    7.2. permit all seats in at least one chamber of the national legislature to be freely contested in a popular vote;

    7.3. guarantee universal and equal suffrage to adult citizens;

    ...

Protocol to the Convention for the Protection of Human Rights and Fundamental Freedoms

Article 3 – Right to free elections

The High Contracting Parties undertake to hold free elections at reasonable intervals by secret ballot, under conditions which will ensure the free expression of the opinion of the people in the choice of the legislature.

Inter-American Democratic Charter

Article 2

The effective exercise of representative democracy is the basis for the rule of law and of the constitutional regimes of the member states of the Organization of American States. Representative democracy is strengthened and deepened by permanent, ethical, and responsible participation of the citizenry within a legal framework conforming to the respective constitutional order.

Article 3

Essential elements of representative democracy include, inter alia, respect for human rights and fundamental freedoms, access to and the exercise of power in accordance with the rule of law, the holding of periodic, free, and fair elections based on secret balloting and universal suffrage as an expression of the sovereignty of the people, the pluralistic system of political parties and organizations, and the separation of powers and independence of the branches of government.

Article 5

The strengthening of political parties and other political organizations is a priority for democracy. Special attention will be paid to the problems associated with the high cost of election campaigns and the establishment of a balanced and transparent system for their financing.

American Convention on Human Rights

Article 23. Right to participate in government

1. Every citizen shall enjoy the following rights and opportunities:

   (a) to take part in the conduct of public affairs, directly or through freely chosen representatives;

   (b) to vote and to be elected in genuine periodic elections, which shall be by universal and equal suffrage and by secret ballot that guarantees the free expression of the will of the voters; and

   (c) to have access, under general conditions of equality, to the public service of his country.

2. The law may regulate the exercise of the rights and opportunities referred to in the preceding paragraph only on the basis of age, nationality, residence, language, education, civil and mental capacity, or sentencing by a competent court in criminal proceedings.

American Declaration on the Rights and Duties of Man

Article XX

Every person having legal capacity is entitled to participate in the government of his country, directly or through his representatives, and to take part in popular elections, which shall be by secret ballot, and shall be honest, periodic and free.

Article XXXII

It is the duty of every person to vote in the popular elections of the country of which he is a national, when he is legally capable of doing so.

African Charter on Democracy, Elections and Governance

Article 4

1. State Parties shall commit themselves to promote democracy, the principle of the rule of law and human rights.
2. State Parties shall recognize popular participation through universal suffrage as the inalienable right of the people.

Principles and Guidelines Governing Democratic Elections (of the Southern African Development Community)

4.1 Member States shall invite SADC Electoral Observation Missions (SEOMs) to observe their elections, based on the provisions of the SADC Treaty, the Protocol on Politics, Defence and Security Cooperation and the *SADC Principles and Guidelines Governing Democratic Elections*. To this end, Member States hereby commit themselves to upholding the following "Principles for Conducting Democratic Elections" in the furtherance of democratic elections in the SADC region:

4.1.1 Encourage the full participation of all citizens in democratic and development processes;

4.1.2 Ensure that all citizens enjoy fundamental freedoms and human rights, including freedom of association, assembly and expression;

Declaration on the Principles Governing Democratic Elections in Africa (of the African Union)

IV. Elections: rights and obligations

We reaffirm the following rights and obligations under which democratic elections are conducted:

1. Every citizen shall have the right to participate freely in the government of his or her country, either directly or through freely elected representatives in accordance with the provisions of the law.
2. Every citizen has the right to fully participate in the electoral processes of the country, including the right to vote or be voted for, according to the laws of the country and as guaranteed by the Constitution, without any kind of discrimination.

...

Protocol A/SP1/12/01 on Democracy and Good Governance Supplementary to the Protocol relating to the Mechanism for Conflict Prevention, Management, Resolution, Peacekeeping and Security (of the Economic Community of West African States)

Article 1

The following shall be declared as constitutional principles shared by all Member States:

...

(b) Every accession to power must be made through free, fair and transparent elections.

...

(d) Popular participation in decision-making, strict adherence to democratic principles and decentralization of power at all levels of governance.

Article 2

1. No substantial modification shall be made to the electoral laws in the last six (6) months before the elections, except with the consent of a majority of Political actors.
2. All the elections shall be organised on the dates or at periods fixed by the Constitution or the electoral laws.
3. Member States shall take all appropriate measures to ensure that women have equal rights with men to vote and be voted for in elections, to participate in the formulation of government policies and the implementation thereof and to hold public offices and perform public functions at all levels of governance.

Article 3

The bodies responsible for organising the elections shall be independent or neutral and shall have the confidence of all the political actors. Where necessary, appropriate national consultations shall be organised to determine the nature and the structure of the bodies.

Article 4

1. Each ECOWAS Member State shall ensure the establishment of a reliable registry of births and deaths. A central registry shall be established in each Member State.

2. Member States shall cooperate in this area with a view to exchanging experiences and where necessary providing technical assistance to each other in the production of reliable voters' lists.

Article 5

The voters' lists shall be prepared in a transparent and reliable manner, with the collaboration of the political parties and voters who may have access to them whenever the need arises.

Article 6

The preparation and conduct of elections and the announcement of results shall be done in a transparent manner.

Article 7

Adequate arrangements shall be made to hear and dispose of all petitions relating to the conduct of elections and announcement of results.

Article 8

Member States shall use the services of civil society organisations involved in electoral matters to educate and enlighten the public on the need for peaceful elections devoid of all acts of violence.

Article 9

The party and/or candidate who loses the elections shall concede defeat to the political party and/or candidate finally declared the winner, following the guidelines and within the deadline stipulated by the law.

Article 10

All holders of power at all levels shall refrain from acts of intimidation or harassment against defeated candidates or their supporters.

Revised Treaty of the Economic Community of West African States

Article 4. Fundamental principles

The high contracting parties, in pursuit of the objectives stated in Article 3 of this Treaty, solemnly affirm and declare their adherence to the following principles:

...

(j) promotion and consolidation of a democratic system of governance in each Member State as envisaged by the Declaration of Political Principles adopted in Abuja on 6 July, 1991; and

...

African Charter on Human and Peoples' Rights

Article 13

1. Every citizen shall have the right to participate freely in the government of his country, either directly or through freely chosen representatives in accordance with the provisions of the law.
2. Every citizen shall have the right of equal access to the public service of his country.
3. Every individual shall have the right of access to public property and services in strict equality of all persons before the law.

Arab Charter on Human Rights

Article 24

Every citizen has the right:

1. To freely pursue a political activity.
2. To take part in the conduct of public affairs, directly or through freely chosen representatives.
3. To stand for election or choose his representatives in free and impartial elections, in conditions of equality among all citizens that guarantee the free expression of his will.
4. To the opportunity to gain access, on an equal footing with others, to public office in his country in accordance with the principle of equality of opportunity.

...

ASEAN Human Rights Declaration

Article 25

1. Every person who is a citizen of his or her country has the right to participate in the government of his or her country, either directly or through democratically elected representatives, in accordance with national law.
2. Every citizen has the right to vote in periodic and genuine elections, which should be held by universal and equal suffrage and by secret ballot, guaranteeing the free expression of the will of the electors, in accordance with national law.

B. Non-discrimination and equal access to participation

Charter of Fundamental Rights of the European Union

Article 21 – Non-discrimination

1. Any discrimination based on any ground such as sex, race, colour, ethnic or social origin, genetic features, language, religion or belief, political or any other opinion, membership of a national minority, property, birth, disability, age or sexual orientation shall be prohibited.

2. Within the scope of application of the Treaty establishing the European Community and of the Treaty on European Union, and without prejudice to the special provisions of those Treaties, any discrimination on grounds of nationality shall be prohibited.

Protocol No. 12 to the Convention for the Protection of Human Rights and Fundamental Freedoms

Article 1 – General prohibition of discrimination

1. The enjoyment of any right set forth by law shall be secured without discrimination on any ground such as sex, race, colour, language, religion, political or other opinion, national or social origin, association with a national minority, property, birth or other status.

2. No one shall be discriminated against by any public authority on any ground such as those mentioned in paragraph 1.

Framework Convention for the Protection of National Minorities (of the Council of Europe)

Article 15

The Parties shall create the conditions necessary for the effective participation of persons belonging to national minorities in cultural, social and economic life and in public affairs, in particular those affecting them.

Convention on the Participation of Foreigners in Public Life at Local Level (of the Council of Europe)

Chapter C – Right to vote in local authority elections

Article 6

1. Each Party undertakes, subject to the provisions of Article 9, paragraph 1, to grant to every foreign resident the right to vote and to stand for election in local authority elections, provided that he fulfils the same legal requirements as apply to nationals and furthermore has been a lawful and habitual resident in the State concerned for the 5 years preceding the elections.
2. However, a Contracting State may declare, when depositing its instrument of ratification, acceptance, approval or accession, that it intends to confine the application of paragraph 1 to the right to vote only.

Convention for the Protection of Human Rights and Fundamental Freedoms (European Convention on Human Rights)

Article 14 – Prohibition of discrimination

The enjoyment of the rights and freedoms set forth in this Convention shall be secured without discrimination on any ground such as sex, race, colour, language, religion, political or other opinion, national or social origin, association with a national minority, property, birth or other status.

Inter-American Democratic Charter

Article 9

The elimination of all forms of discrimination, especially gender, ethnic and race discrimination, as well as diverse forms of intolerance, the promotion and protection of human rights of indigenous peoples and migrants, and respect for ethnic, cultural and religious diversity in the Americas contribute to strengthening democracy and citizen participation.

Article 28

States shall promote the full and equal participation of women in the political structures of their countries as a fundamental element in the promotion and exercise of a democratic culture.

American Convention on Human Rights

Article 1. Obligation to respect rights

1. The States Parties to this Convention undertake to respect the rights and freedoms recognized herein and to ensure to all persons subject to their jurisdiction the free and full exercise of those rights and freedoms, without any discrimination for reasons of race, color, sex, language, religion, political or other opinion, national or social origin, economic status, birth, or any other social condition.
2. For the purposes of this Convention, "person" means every human being.

Article 24. Right to equal protection

All persons are equal before the law. Consequently, they are entitled, without discrimination, to equal protection of the law.

Inter-American Convention on the Granting of Political Rights to Women

Article 1

The High Contracting Parties agree that the right to vote and to be elected to national office shall not be denied or abridged by reason of sex.

SADC Protocol on Gender and Development

Article 13 – Participation

1. States Parties shall adopt specific legislative measures and other strategies to enable women to have equal opportunities with men to participate in all electoral processes including the administration of elections and voting.

...

Protocol to the African Charter on Human and Peoples' Rights on the Rights of Women in Africa

Article 9 – Right to participation in the political and decision-making process

1. States Parties shall take specific positive action to promote participative governance and the equal participation of women in the political life of their countries through affirmative action, enabling national legislation and other measures to ensure that:

(a) Women participate without any discrimination in all elections;

(b) Women are represented equally at all levels with men in all electoral processes;

(c) Women are equal partners with men at all levels of development and implementation of State policies and development programmes.

2. States Parties shall ensure increased and effective representation and participation of women at all levels of decision-making.

African Charter on Human and Peoples' Rights

Article 2

Every individual shall be entitled to the enjoyment of the rights and freedoms recognized and guaranteed in the present Charter without distinction of any kind such as race, ethnic group, colour, sex, language, religion, political or any other opinion, national and social origin, fortune, birth or other status.

Article 3

1. Every individual shall be equal before the law.
2. Every individual shall be entitled to equal protection of the law.

Arab Charter on Human Rights

Article 3

...

3. Men and women are equal in respect of human dignity, rights and obligations within the framework of the positive discrimination established in favour of women by the Islamic Shariah, other divine laws and by applicable laws and legal instruments. Accordingly, each State party pledges to take all the requisite measures to guarantee equal opportunities and effective equality between men and women in the enjoyment of all the rights set out in this Charter.

C. Right to self-determination

African Charter on Human and Peoples' Rights

Article 19

All peoples shall be equal; they shall enjoy the same respect and shall have the same rights. Nothing shall justify the domination of a people by another.

Article 20

1. All peoples shall have the right to existence. They shall have the unquestionable and inalienable right to self-determination. They shall freely determine their political status and shall pursue their economic and social development according to the policy they have freely chosen.

2. Colonized or oppressed peoples shall have the right to free themselves from the bonds of domination by resorting to any means recognized by the international community.

3. All peoples shall have the right to the assistance of the States Parties to the present Charter in their liberation struggle against foreign domination, be it political, economic or cultural.

Arab Charter on Human Rights

Article 2

1. All peoples have the right of self-determination and to control over their natural wealth and resources, and the right to freely choose their political system and to freely pursue their economic, social and cultural development.

ANNEX III
UNITED NATIONS HUMAN RIGHTS SYSTEM

1. The United Nations human rights system is composed of mechanisms with monitoring mandates derived from the Charter of the United Nations (so-called Charter-based bodies) and bodies created under the international human rights treaties and made up of independent experts (so-called treaty-based bodies or treaty bodies).

A. Charter-based bodies

2. The Charter-based bodies are the Human Rights Council, its universal periodic review and its special procedures.

1. Human Rights Council

3. The Human Rights Council is an intergovernmental body within the United Nations system made up of 47 States, which are elected by the General Assembly through a simple majority vote. The Council is the principal body within the United Nations system responsible for strengthening the promotion and protection of human rights and for addressing and taking action on human rights violations worldwide. The Council was created by the General Assembly on 15 March 2006 through its adoption of resolution 60/251. The Council meets at the United Nations Office at Geneva for 10 weeks a year and has the ability to discuss all thematic human rights issues and situations that require its attention throughout the year.

4. The Council can adopt decisions, statements and resolutions with or without a recorded vote. To adopt a draft text through a vote, it must enjoy the support of a majority of the members of the Council. Only Council members are able to vote. The decisions of the Council are not legally binding. To date, the Council has adopted more than 1,750 texts to address a wide range of thematic and country-specific human rights issues.

2. Universal periodic review

5. The Human Rights Council's universal periodic review is a unique process that involves a review of the human rights records of all 193 States members of the United Nations once every four and a half years.

6. Every year, some 42 States are reviewed, receiving an average of 180 recommendations each. Reviewed States are then expected to indicate

which recommendations they support and to report on measures and steps taken to implement them. The universal periodic review is one of many entry points for United Nations engagement on human rights and the recommendations explicitly supported by a Government constitute the most consensual one. As a peer review process, recommendations from the universal periodic review are made by fellow States and complement or reiterate other recommendations issued by United Nations expert human rights bodies, such as the treaty bodies, the special procedures of the Human Rights Council and OHCHR.[1]

3. Special procedures

7. The Human Rights Council's special procedure mandate holders are made up of special rapporteurs, independent experts and working groups who are appointed by the Council and who serve in their personal capacity. Special procedures carry out country visits; act on individual cases and concerns of a broader, structural nature by sending communications to States and other actors, bringing alleged violations or abuses to their attention; conduct thematic studies and convene expert consultations; contribute to the development of international human rights standards; engage in advocacy; raise public awareness; and provide advice for technical cooperation.

8. The mandate holders are independent of any Government or organization and serve in their individual capacity. They report to the Council on their findings and recommendations, as well as to the General Assembly. At times, they are the only mechanism alerting the international community to certain human rights issues. Special procedures base their conclusions and recommendations on objective assessments of human rights situations. Special procedures do not have the power or authority to enforce their views or recommendations.

9. As of September 2020, there were 80 active special procedure mandate holders for 55 mandates – 44 thematic mandates and 11 country-specific mandates.

B. Treaty bodies

10. There are 10 human rights treaty bodies that monitor implementation of the core international human rights treaties, namely:

(a) The Committee on the Elimination of Racial Discrimination;

(b) The Committee on Economic, Social and Cultural Rights;

---

[1] See www.ohchr.org/Documents/HRBodies/UPR/UPR_Practical_Guidance.pdf.

(c) The Human Rights Committee;

(d) The Committee on the Elimination of Discrimination against Women;

(e) The Committee against Torture;

(f) The Committee on the Rights of the Child;

(g) The Committee on Migrant Workers;

(h) The Subcommittee on Prevention of Torture and Other Cruel, Inhuman or Degrading Treatment or Punishment;

(i) The Committee on the Rights of Persons with Disabilities;

(j) The Committee on Enforced Disappearances.

11. The treaty bodies perform a number of functions in accordance with the provisions of the treaties that established them. These include consideration of States parties' periodic reports, consideration of individual complaints and adoption of general comments or recommendations interpreting treaty provisions.[2]

1. Consideration of States parties' reports

12. When a State ratifies a treaty, it assumes a legal obligation to implement the rights recognized in that treaty. In addition to its obligation to implement the substantive provisions of the treaty, each State party is also under an obligation to submit periodic reports to the relevant treaty body on how the rights are being implemented.

13. The treaty body concerned reviews States parties' reports, and may receive information on a country's human rights situation from other sources, including national human rights institutions, civil society organizations, both international and national, United Nations entities, other intergovernmental organizations, and professional groups and academic institutions. In the light of all the information available, the relevant treaty body examines the report in the presence of a delegation from the State party. The treaty body then publishes its concerns and recommendations, referred to as its "concluding observations".

---

[2] For more information on the treaty bodies, see OHCHR, *The United Nations Human Rights Treaty System*, Fact Sheet No. 30/Rev.1 (New York and Geneva, 2012).

2. Consideration of individual complaints.

14. Six of the treaty bodies (the Committee on the Elimination of Racial Discrimination, the Human Rights Committee, the Committee on the Elimination of Discrimination against Women, the Committee against Torture, the Committee on the Rights of Persons with Disabilities and the Committee on Enforced Disappearances) can, under certain conditions, receive petitions from individuals claiming that their rights under the respective treaty have been violated by a State party to that treaty. Once a committee declares that a complaint is admissible, the committee proceeds to consider it on its merits, stating the reasons for concluding that a violation has or has not occurred under the applicable treaty provisions.

15. The committees' decisions represent an authoritative interpretation of the respective treaties. They contain recommendations to the State party in question but they are not legally binding. All committees have developed procedures to monitor whether States parties have implemented their recommendations (so-called follow-up procedures), since they consider that, by accepting the complaint procedures, State parties have also accepted to respect the committees' findings. The resulting body of decisions may guide States, civil society and individuals in interpreting the contemporary meaning of these treaties.[3]

3. General comments and recommendations

16. Each of the treaty bodies publishes its interpretation of the provisions of its respective treaty in the form of general comments or recommendations. The general comments and recommendations provide additional information of a more elaborate nature on how the treaties should be implemented. They cover a wide range of subjects, from the comprehensive interpretation of substantive provisions, such as the right to freedom of expression or the right to participate in public affairs, to general guidance on the information that should be submitted in States parties' reports relating to specific articles of the treaties.

17. General comments and recommendations have also dealt with wider, cross-cutting issues, such as the role of national human rights institutions, the rights of persons with disabilities, violence against women and the rights of minorities. They are all available from the OHCHR website (www.ohchr.org).

---

[3] For more information on treaty bodies complaint procedures, see OHCHR, *Individual Complaint Procedures under the United Nations Human Rights Treaties*, Fact Sheet No. 7/Rev.2 (New York and Geneva, 2013).